Motivating People

By

Dayle M. Smith, Ph.D.
Georgetown University

All inquiries should be addressed to:
Barron's Educational Series, Inc.
250 Wireless Boulevard
Hauppauge, New York 11788

Library of Congress Catalog Card Number 91-677

International Standard Book No. 0-8120-4673-0

Library of Congress Cataloging in Publication Data
Smith, Dayle M.
    Motivating people / by Dayle M. Smith.
      p. cm. — (Barron's business success series)
    Includes bibliographical references.
    ISBN 0-8120-4673-0
    1. Employee motivation. I. Title. II. Series
HF5549.5.M63S62 1991
658.3'14—dc20   91-677
                                     CIP

PRINTED IN THE UNITED STATES OF AMERICA
234 9770 98765432

CONTENTS

PREFACE

I t isn't possible to thank by name the hundreds of my colleagues, business associates, students, and friends who have helped me understand the nature and importance of motivation in business life. I must, however, single out several individuals well-known for their ability to motivate and even inspire others: at Georgetown University School of Business Administration, Professors Annette Shelby, Karen Gaertner, Dennis Quinn, Mary Culnan, Elizabeth Cooper-Martin, and Bill Gardner; at the University of Southern California, Professors Mary Ann von Glinow, Barry Leskin, Tom Housel, Carol Shuherk, Michael Cody, Margaret McLaughlin, and David Braaten; at Arizona State University, Caren Siehl and David Bowen; at Companion Life Insurance, Roberta and Jerry Natelson; at Artex Knitting Mills, Arthur Pottash; at Critikon, Cindy Bryan, Hinda Smith, and Gary Trotter; at Lucky Stores, Inc., Cherie Kester; at the *Los Angeles Times,* Bill Bradley; at General Electric, Jane Schnor; at R.A. Bell Associates, Bob Bell; at Free Spirit, Inc., Lewis Smith, Owen Smith, and Charles Gerson; at Rachlin and Ain, CPA, Clifford Ain; at U.S. Customs Department, Gary Rothschild; and at Allied Realty, Jean Dorset.

Finally, my heartfelt thanks to my best personal motivators, my family.

Dedicated with love to my husband and best friend, Art.

INTRODUCTION

Let's start with you and me.

You're considering whether to read this book. I want to motivate you to do so.

But where does such motivation begin?

With you and your needs. Perhaps you supervise people who just aren't giving their best to the job. In fact, they may be thinking of new ways to give their worst to the job.

Or you may be struggling with your own feelings of burnout and stagnation. Monday mornings tell you that things just aren't right in your work life.

In either case, you want to know how to light a fire to rekindle some enthusiasm for work. You want employees to *want* to, not *have* to. You may want the same thing for yourself.

This short book sums up the brightest and best ideas on motivation from academic research and corporate experience. But be warned: there's no one answer or motivation trick that will convert chuggers to chargers.

Instead, there are many answers to fit the differing needs of real people. You'll meet ten of these people in the chapters of this book. We'll analyze their work attitudes and experiences to understand the specific motivational principles that fit them best. At the end of each chapter, we'll sum up these principles as Management Tips you can begin using today.

So that's my pitch: read this book to understand what different people reach for and why—in short, what motivates them.

Only slightly disguised among the people in this book, you may find yourself as well. I'm in there. So's my boss.

That should motivate him to read the book. How about you?

CHAPTER 1

WHAT DO YOU NEED?

Motivators and Your "Must Haves"

We human beings have an inborn order, or hierarchy, for what we want.

Sandra Richfield, 33, has worked for a large midwestern chemical company for four years. She is divorced and has one child, Tammy, age 5.

When I'm asked what I need from work, I usually say, "Money, and more of it." And that's partly true. But I'll give you the long answer, for what it's worth.

About five years ago, just after my daughter was born, I had what women call a sick divorce. I was so miserable in my marriage that I signed anything and everything just to get my ex out of the house and out of my life.

What I was left with was a transportation car, the apartment furniture, a big Visa bill, and a daughter to raise by myself. I had about $600 in savings and no job.

So when I applied to this company as a secretary, it was literally to keep a roof over our heads and food on the table. I remember holding my first paycheck and crying in the restroom for relief and joy. We wouldn't starve. We would get by.

A few months later Tammy came down with bronchitis. Nothing that serious, but we went through a lot of medical tests and several prescriptions. I learned how to turn in bills to my Blue Cross insurance at work.

And I realized that I could get sick and things would be OK. I could go to the dentist, I could take Tammy, and work would pay. I had life insurance and a retirement plan. For the first time in months, I felt safe for both of us.

Work became a big part of my social life. I don't know how it is in other companies, but in mine you pretty much hang out with employees at your same level. I'm friendly with my supervisor and her boss, but they usually have their own circle for lunch and after-work things.

My group is what we jokingly call the "S.S."— Satisfied Secretaries. You see, there are two basic groups of secretaries in the company. There are the "wilders," who seemingly have no responsibilities. A lot of them are just out of school or going part-time, still living at home or off Mom and Dad somehow, with no kids to provide for and a party every other night. This group hates work, and at lunch and breaks they say so. They're funny. Nothing at work is ever right for them. "The windows are dirty," "the parking lot doesn't have enough lights," "the cafeteria coffee is awful." You name it.

Then there's my group. I wouldn't say we love work, but we all rely on our jobs to keep our families going. I have nothing against the other group, but I'm not 18 any more and I can't pretend I am.

A year ago something good happened to me at work. I was promoted to executive assistant, which is one step up from secretary and pays a bit more money. The company actually gave me business cards with my new title; I use them for sales people, suppliers, and others I have to deal with.

I think I can be happy in this position for a long time. My parents are obviously proud of my promotion and feel that their daughter has finally succeeded at

*something. I've gotten to know most of the other
executive assistants in my division, and more and
more, some of us are doing things outside of work.*

*There's no aspect of my present job that I can't
handle and my work evaluations are excellent.
Sometimes my boss asks me to take on projects for her
that are out of my league, and I tell her so. I'd rather
do my own work well than take on someone else's
and do a mediocre job. It took a while, but I think
my boss understands that about me."*

FOLLOW-UP INFORMATION

According to her superiors, Sandra Richfield has the intelligence to move into training for a supervisory position.
When approached with this idea, Sandra tends to pass it
off as a compliment but an impractical option. She explains
her reticence on the basis of her lack of a college degree.
Other supervisors, she says, have more education than
she does. This issue is not an obstacle on the part of
management.

Sandra recently talked her daughter, Tammy, out of
taking dance lessons. "You and I were born with two left
feet, honey," she explained.

MOTIVATORS AT WORK

Sandra Richfield's changing work experiences demonstrate what Abraham Maslow has called a "hierarchy of
needs." In Maslow's view, we human beings have an inborn order, or hierarchy, for what we want. We move
through stages of need, progressing to later stages only
when earlier stages have been satisfied.

As illustrated in Maslow's familiar pyramid of needs,
Sandra Richfield (and the rest of us) must first satisfy our
physiological needs (food, shelter, clothing) before we can
contemplate or act upon other priorities. You may note a
small but significant change in the appearance of Maslow's

Hierarchy of Needs here: the rounded corners are meant to suggest that the pyramid of needs, far from being a rigid structure, is actually an "elastic bag." Its shape can stretch and change to reflect the relative strength of felt needs.

When Sandra first came to work, for example, her need structure could be well depicted as the structure above. Uppermost on her mind were physiological needs. She had the rent to pay and food to buy. Her baby needed shoes. For the first month or two of employment, in fact, Sandra was probably motivated to perform well primarily by her fear of not meeting these physiological needs.

For this reason, many companies have 60- to 90-day probation periods at the beginning of a person's employment. This policy acts as a not-so-subtle reminder that employment may come to a sudden end if job criteria aren't met. During her first weeks on the job, Sandra got to work on time and kept her nose to the grindstone, not out of a love for work or office camaraderie but to fulfill her physiological needs.

Notice, however, how Sandra's personal pyramid of needs began to change as time passed. As she became less and less afraid of losing her job, a new set of needs took prominence in her mind: the need for security.

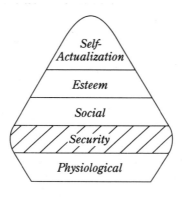

Once the basic matters of food, shelter, and clothing were handled, Sandra began to focus on the "what ifs" of life. What if my child or I gets sick? What if we need dental care? What will I eventually do about retirement? When asking questions such as these, Sandra is in the grip of security motivators. Her benefits package looms large to her as the most important aspect of her worklife. In this stage, she would probably ignore other motivators—a higher salary from a competing company, for example—if they were not accompanied by a comparable benefits package.

But, like the physiological stage, the security stage occupies Sandra's attention less and less as time passes. She feels secure about her benefits package; in other words, she satisfies her security needs. This is not to say that she no longer feels a need for security. Rather, its strength in her spectrum of needs diminishes. The dimensions of her personal need pyramid reflect new concerns.

Now social needs gain prominence in Sandra's thinking and feeling. She finds real pleasure in her work friendships with the "satisfied secretaries" group. She wouldn't think of quitting her job, even for more money elsewhere, because "I would miss the people."

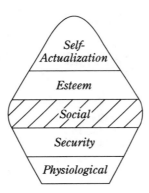

Notice that Sandra hasn't chosen co-workers at random to satisfy her social needs. As the work of Elton Mayo shows, we all tend to seek membership in groups that confirm our own values and validate our own experiences. As one writer has quipped, "Misery not only loves company. Misery loves miserable company."

Sandra, fortunately, is not miserable in her worklife. But she does forgo friendship with the younger, party set of secretaries. Her social needs can be fulfilled only when she surrounds herself with others who understand and generally approve her day-to-day life choices.

There is one interesting footnote about the party set of secretaries. As the research of Clayton Alderfer shows, we may all leap back to lower stages of need when experiencing frustration at higher need levels. The party secretaries, for example, weren't able to fulfill their social needs at work—the office was "boring, stupid, dead." As a result of such frustration, lower-stage physiological and security needs begin to resurface: "I keep watching the paper for news about a takeover of this company—we could all be out on the street!" (physiological needs). "They've got to install better lighting in the parking lot" (security needs). In other words, the shape of the party secretaries' need pyramid can be distorted by frustration to look like this:

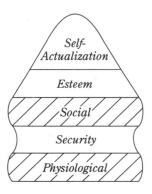

Once secure in her social life, Sandra seeks to fulfill her need for esteem. Now foremost in her mind are questions about her relative prestige for people that matter to her. What do her mother and father think of her position at work? What does daughter Tammy think about Mommy's occupation? For that matter, what does Sandra herself think about being a secretary? Is this "it"?

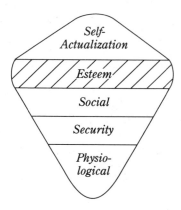

During the esteem stage of need, Sandra is motivated by anything—a job title, a business card, a nameplate on her desk—that bespeaks status. Like many bank vice presidents, at this stage she would ignore money motivators for the sake of the all-important job title.

It's interesting to note what would happen, though, if Sandra's social group felt that she was snubbing them in her pursuit of status. If this group stopped fulfilling Sandra's social needs (in effect, abandoned her), Sandra would undoubtedly turn back from her esteem needs to the previous stage of social needs. She would refuse the motivator of promotion, for example, if it meant ostracization by her former friends.

Like Sandra, many rising professionals find themselves oscillating between social needs and esteem needs. The warm, secure feeling of being part of the group often seems to come with strings attached: you can be one of us so long as you share our values and hardships. Changes in status may bring changes in friends — and hard choices.

Sandra, for example, finds herself moving on to a new set of work associates as her prestige needs are fulfilled. She now has lunch more often with the executive assistants than with her previous group, the "satisfied secretaries." Sandra probably reassures her former co-workers that "I really want to get together to catch up." She may explain away her new lunch companions on the basis of work: "We have to meet through lunch to keep up with things." The truth, of course, is that Sandra is trying to harmonize her social needs with her esteem needs. She knows she doesn't want to have one without the other. Therefore, she's building a new social life to match her growing need to make people proud of her, and to be proud of herself.

Sandra fulfills her own personal esteem needs by a new job title and the relative social distinction it carries with it in the office place. She now turns to her need for self-actualization—the "what's-my-life-about" question.

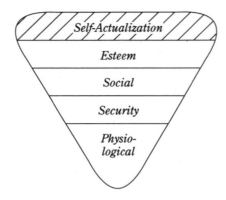

In this stage, Sandra cares intensely about her competence and personal achievements. She wants to master the skills of her occupation—not, importantly, to impress others but to fulfill her own need for control and expertise. She wants to *achieve*, to score high on her own personal chart of possible accomplishments.

When seeking self-actualization, Sandra is motivated primarily by tasks and relationships that are neither too difficult nor too easy. She may relish the idea of learning desktop publishing, for example, or helping to revamp the office filing system. She probably would not be motivated by the chance to help install a voice-mail system in the workplace. Even if the necessary electrical and wiring skills could be taught to Sandra within a few days, she would see this task as "beyond my limits."

In a fascinating human study, Harvard University researcher David C. McClelland asked participants to throw rings over a peg from any distance they chose. Obviously, a person could get all the rings onto the peg by standing right beside it. By contrast, a person might never get a single ring onto the peg by standing too far away from it. The vast majority of participants instinctively sought out their own "interest range"—the distance away that assured some success but also promised challenge and risk.

Sandra has chosen a rather close range from which to toss her personal rings for self-actualization. She has apparently told her boss on several occasions that some job challenges "aren't in my league." Sadly, her self-imposed limitations are being passed along to her daughter: "You and I were born with two left feet, honey."

As Sandra's employer, you may regret the low ceiling of achievement under which Sandra has chosen to lead her professional life. The question is how can you raise that ceiling—in effect, how to help Sandra find pleasure in higher levels of achievement—without arousing unmanageable levels of fear within her: "My boss isn't satisfied with me" (worries based on esteem needs). "If I fail at this, everyone will mock me" (worries based on esteem and social needs).

In your efforts to motivate Sandra, remember the rings-and-peg experiment. Your goal is to help Sandra find excitement and challenge in moving back farther and farther from the peg. All the while, however, she must have a relatively secure sense of her own competence; she has to ring the peg often. In practical terms, therefore, you would ease Sandra into new job tasks gradually. You would remind her about accomplishments in new areas and emphasize achievement rather than failure. You would highlight the excitement of new challenges in such a way that does not arouse her fears of losing her social group or risking embarrassing failure.

PRACTICAL MANAGEMENT TIPS

Several insights for managers emerge from an understanding of the hierarchy of needs.

1. Motivators have meaning only in relation to the strength of a given need as perceived by the individual employee. At some stages, the lure of money may be almost meaningless; at other stages, it may seem all-important.

2. Managers can understand their employee's needs only by listening to and observing them.

3. Employees will take on new challenges only when their other needs remain relatively satisfied. The increased status of new job responsibilities and titles may be unattractive to employees concerned primarily about social relations.

4. Managers tend to project their own stage of need onto their employees. A manager obsessed with upper levels of self-actualization, for example, may not understand why subordinates resist attending a two-week seminar on advanced programming skills. Don't they want to be more competent than their co-workers? Don't they want to master sophisticated skills? Perhaps not. These may be motivating values for the manager, but not for the subordinate.

CHAPTER 2

WHAT DO YOU EXPECT?

Motivators and Your Crystal Ball

Our efforts intensify to the extent that we believe goal-fulfillment to be possible.

Todd Mallek, 40, sells heavy industrial equipment for a major industrial broker on the West Coast. He is married without children and travels two weeks a month on average.

My job is pretty much like Las Vegas: you spin the wheel and hope for a major score. If it doesn't come, you spin again. As long as it takes.

When I started in this position six years ago, I got discouraged too easily. I remember one time in particular. I flew all the way up to Seattle from L.A. to meet a prospective customer. The guy had me spend most of the day with him going around to different job sites and looking at various pieces of equipment he already owned. It was typical Seattle weather—cold rain—and I came back with the flu.

And all for nothing. He bought from my competitor the next day for the same price I was offering him. I just about quit that day.

But then there are the good days, when orders and commissions come in one on top of each other. Those are the days that keep me going.

Now my philosophy is this: get out there and put in the legwork meeting new customers and understanding their operations. Eight contacts out of ten may lead nowhere, but if the remaining two buy equipment, it's fat city on payday.

Travelling around as I do, I hear about job possibilities with other companies. But the reason I stay here is the upside potential. What else could I be doing that would net me six figures in a good year?

I tell the new sales people that there's only one trick to having a really good year: avoid the post-honeymoon syndrome. This is when you wine and dine a new customer to the point of his or her first purchase or two, then gradually lose interest as you pursue new customers. Customers are never "in the bag," I tell our sales force, and you shouldn't treat them as if they were.

Since I'm the senior person now and usually hit the top numbers each year, the company is having me do some of the sales training for the new guys. It cuts into my own calls a bit, but I enjoy talking about something I know so well. And, although the company doesn't know it, I'm going to hit them up one of these days for a bonus based on the gross sales of the people I train.

FOLLOW-UP INFORMATION

Todd Mallek is under treatment for a chronic ulcer condition. He worries privately that his health won't sustain a continuing schedule of heavy travel. His company, however, has been holding him up lately as a model of sorts for the rest of the sales staff. Todd wonders what lies ahead for him in his forties and fifties. He likes to have a plan for his life. But the ulcer has raised many unanswered questions.

"I'd rather burn out than rust out," Todd tells himself. He has not followed his doctor's advice to reduce stress.

MOTIVATORS AT WORK

One important goal for Todd Mallek is making the sale. His physiological needs (food, shelter, clothing), economic security, social relations, sense of esteem, and other factors all depend in part on closing the deal.

To achieve this end, Todd is willing to engage in a period of goal-directed activity. Note that this activity (which can include business travel, product presentations, phone calls, and so forth) does not in itself fulfill Todd's needs listed above. In fact, if he were only to engage in goal-directed activities without ever achieving the goal, he would be looked upon as a failure—a well-intentioned but unsuccessful sales person.

Early in his career, Todd perceived the relation of goal-directed activity to goal fulfillment in this way:

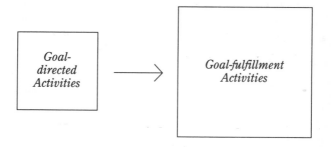

At this initial period, he simply couldn't bear to put too much legwork into a sale; he had to see "results" (goal fulfillment) to keep his confidence up.

With experience, however, Todd now is content with a different allocation of goal-directed activity to goal fulfillment. In other words, he is more sure of his eventual success and therefore is willing to undergo long periods of goal-directed activity without actual fulfillment.

Todd's hard-won sense of patience and confidence can be attributed in part to the powers of visualization and memory. Todd carries within himself powerful and stim-

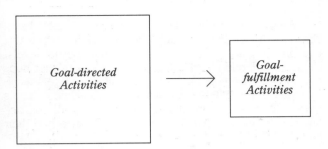

ulating memories about past sales. He remembers holding large commission checks in his hand. He recalls the loud applause when he was recognized as Salesperson of the Year. He sees the sales achievement plaques decorating his wall.

In all of these ways, Todd participates in imaginative goal fulfillment during goal-directed activity. This is not to say that imaginative goal fulfillment pays the mortgage. In a now-famous budget confrontation with California professors, then-Governor Jerry Brown told professors seeking a raise that they should consider themselves paid in "psychic dollars" due to the prestige and social privilege of their positions. One professor then inquired if his state taxes could be paid in these psychic dollars. The governor's response is not a matter of record.

Todd Mallek's motivation, in sum, is based largely on his expectations. The expectancy theories of motivation maintain that most of our actions are based not on receiving actual rewards or avoiding actual pain but instead on our expected (i.e., imagined) versions of those positive or negative payoffs.

Our efforts intensify to the extent that we believe goal-fulfillment to be possible. If Todd sniffs out a possible sale, he will "go for it" with all his energy. But as soon as he concludes that the sale is not possible (perhaps because of a competitor's lower bid), he may withdraw completely.

What motivates Todd, in a word, is the chase. David C. McClelland and John W. Atkinson studied this phenomenon across industries and employment levels. Contrary to intuition, they discovered that motivation does not continue to increase as the probability of goal-fulfillment nears 100 percent. In fact, as goal-fulfillment seems more and more a "sure thing," motivation tends to slack off. McClelland and Atkinson portray this pattern in their famous "50 Percent Curve":

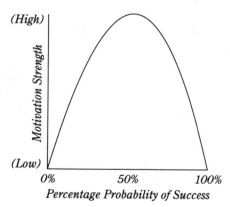

Motivation in Relation to Probability of Success

As depicted here, motivation rises as goal-fulfillment moves from improbable toward probable, but then begins to fall as goal-fulfillment begins to seem inevitable.

Members of a football team, for example, play their hearts out as long as the outcome is undecided. But as soon as failure or success is guaranteed, players may simply go through the motions of the sport.

In Todd Mallek's words, this is the "post-honeymoon syndrome"—the dip in motivation after the courtship has won the prize. As Todd tries to teach his proteges, this syndrome can be resisted by recognizing it and redoubling efforts past the 50 percent point.

Victor Vroom has helped a generation of managers understand the inner workings of expectancy motivation. Vroom points out that expectancy involves three key factors:

If you believe that your effort affects your performance

(and)

If you believe that your performance determines predictable outcomes

(and)

If you believe that you value those outcomes

. . . then you will be motivated to expend maximum or near-maximum effort.

In Todd's case, he first expects that his personal investment of energy (in the form of sales visits, travel, phone calls, and so forth) will affect his performance as a sales person. "No one has success just handed to him," Todd likes to say. Second, he expects that his performance will lead to predictable outcomes. His contract with the company, for instance, specifies that he will be paid a certain commission rate per sale. Finally, Todd knows that he values both the financial rewards and the prestige of being a top sales person.

But remove any one of Vroom's three components and motivation evaporates. Let's say, for example, that Todd felt his sales were a matter of luck, not effort. Or imagine that the company simply wouldn't pay him his earned commissions. In either case, Todd's motivation to work would virtually disappear. Finally, imagine that Todd (perhaps because of some spiritual conversion) eschews money, the material world and all its trappings. If work outcomes lose their meaning, motivation to achieve them ceases.

This is precisely the motivational sinkhole into which many urban employees find themselves sinking. Their ostensible rewards—a salary, let's say, of $50,000 per year—ceases to have meaning when housing costs skyrocket, childcare expenses top $4,000 (1990 average), and crime rises. The "reward" aspect of the green paper symbols received in the pay envelope begins to pale; the dollars buy less and less satisfaction.

Employers in less commercially intense regions have learned to capitalize on this reality for motivational purposes. "Come to Kansas," one employment ad reads, "where a good salary still buys a great house." As economic imbalances increase among regions, many employees find themselves trapped beneath an area's reward ceiling. A talented agricultural chemist in Montana can't afford to accept his company's offer of a transfer to the home office in New York. His spacious home and other amenities couldn't be recreated in New York for twice or three times his salary.

One final aspect of expectancy theory involves the *availability* of necessary environmental factors. I can believe that my effort to sell freezers to Eskimos will affect my sales performance; and I can believe that my company will pay me for every freezer sold; finally, I can believe that I'd love those dollars. But if the subzero environment makes freezers unnecessary, my motivational supports fall like a house of cards.

Entrepreneurs often face this motivational Waterloo. Without adequate market studies, they assemble a ground-floor staff and set off with great enthusiasm to franchise the world (or other sales goal). When the enterprise fails to achieve results, the boss too often—and incorrectly—examines only the three motivational components: Why aren't my employees giving their best? (the effort-performance component) Do I have to increase salaries and commissions? (the performance-outcomes component) Do they want something besides money? (the outcomes-value component).

The culprit all along may be availability. The region or economy may be to blame, not the motivational level or sincerity of the employees. A CEO's dollars, in other words, should sometimes be spent in market research and development rather than employee pep talks and pep pills in their various forms.

Todd Mallek's boss, for example, may soon have to confront a specialized case of availability with regard to Todd's chronic ulcer condition. No matter what Todd's expectations, his own health environment may prove a limiting factor to his further achievement. Recognizing this, Todd's boss may opt to use Todd's expertise for in-house training rather than subjecting him to the continuing rigors of the road.

In doing so, Todd's boss will have to walk an interesting motivational tightrope. Todd, after all, expects his performance to lead to valuable outcomes. To date, Todd has defined those valuable outcomes in terms of dollars and prestige as a top salesperson. Todd's boss will have to convince Todd that an increase in his prestige (his visibility in-house as the ultimate salesperson) more than makes up for a dip in his economic rewards.

In summary, anything is possible in Todd's future, limited only by his health. His motivation to work depends directly upon his expectations, which may be fulfilled by the company in both tangible and intangible ways. In a word, we work because we believe, not because we receive.

MANAGEMENT TIPS

Expectancy theories of motivation emphasize the internal world of hopes and dreams more than the external world of money and position. Four practical lessons can be drawn from the Todd Mallek case:

1. Each individual has his or her own set of expectations and beliefs regarding work. These inner forces are their prime motivators for achievement.

2. Managers should not assume that external symbols of value (a high salary, a company car) automatically have personal motivating value for a particular employee.

3. Managers choose motivators based on their knowledge of employees' personal expectations.

4. Managers guard against fall-offs in motivation particularly at the beginning of unpromising tasks and toward the conclusion of "sure-bet" tasks.

CHAPTER 3

ARE YOU GETTING WHAT YOU DESERVE?

*Motivators and
Your Sense of
Fairness*

*We compare what we do and receive
with what others do and receive.*

J.S. Adams

Peggy Woodward, 35, is one of six mid-level managers in the San Francisco office of a commercial credit firm. She is single and has sole caregiving responsibility for her elderly mother.

Am I getting what I deserve at this company? Yes and no.

Yes, for my education (B.A. in Business Administration from Ohio State) and experience, I'm getting a better-than-average salary in this industry. The benefits package is good, and we have a profit-sharing plan that adds a few thousand dollars to my retirement plan each year.

But no, I'm not getting what I deserve when it comes to this specific office and some of the things that have been happening here. Last month, for example, all six of us in the mid-level management range found out about our raises: a five percent raise for each of us across the board.

I went home stunned that day. Any objective observer of the company would have seen that, over the past year, four of us have been working like dogs and the other two—I'll call them Alice and Ruth— have been absolutely loafing.

*Last year my immediate boss, the vice president
of cost accounting, gave us all a sermon about merit
raises—how we would individually be rewarded for
our effort. Like fools, four of us took that message
seriously. We came in early, left late, often skipped
lunches, and even spent some Saturdays on the job.*

*Alice and Ruth, however, found every excuse in
the book to be away from their desks. They each took
their maximum number of sick days, got permission
to attend off-site management seminars, and
generally treated their job as a hobby. On several
occasions, Ruth's people came to me for information
and decisions that she was responsible for.*

*The four of us have agreed that, if the company
won't reward our effort, we won't give it. Alice and
Ruth have apparently set the standard of what it takes to
get a five percent raise here, and that's the standard that
the four of us are going to follow as well.*

*I'm not coming in a minute before nine and I'm
leaving promptly at five, no matter what needs doing.
If the vice president asks me about my change in
work habits, I'll be more than happy to explain—and
I'll have three other managers there to back me up.*

*Either Alice and Ruth have to start pulling their
weight around here, or the company should reward
those of us who do.*

FOLLOW-UP INFORMATION

Peggy Woodward and her mother are active church members. Although she has many friends, Peggy considers her
own social and romantic life on hold so long as her mother
needs care. Last year Peggy underwent psychological
treatment for anxiety-induced panic disorder. With the
help of medication and breathing exercises, she has had
good luck controlling this condition. She is an avid gar-
dener. "We have the only lawn on the street with absolutely no crabgrass," she says.

MOTIVATORS AT WORK

Consider Peggy Woodward's point of view. She has no complaint about her salary or benefits *per se*; in fact, she admits they are better than average for the industry. Nor does she dislike her work tasks in themselves.

What bedevils her, however, is the mismatch between her effort/reward ratio and the effort/reward ratios of some of her peers in the company. She is losing motivation, in other words, because of what she perceives as a lack of equity.

J. Stacy Adams is the father of equity theories of motivation. Inevitably, he says, we compare what we do and receive with what others do and receive. If we feel an inequity as a result of that comparison, that response can become a powerful factor in determining our own motivational levels. As in the case of Peggy Woodward, few other traditional motivators—salary, reputation, meaningful work—can overcome the deep burn that we feel because of perceived inequity.

Adams' equation for equity is straightforward:

$$\frac{\text{my reward}}{\text{my input}} \quad \text{should equal} \quad \frac{\text{your reward}}{\text{your input}}$$

When the sides of the equation balance, we're satisfied and proceed to respond to our usual set of motivators. But when the balance tilts heavily against us, we often act out our frustration and sense of injustice.

These responses can take several forms to restore the balance of the equation. First, we may decide to reduce our input (our effort, involvement, or leadership) to produce what we consider a more equitable effort/reward ratio, and perhaps to "pay back" those who caused the felt inequity in the first place. Second, we may try to make the effort/reward ratio more just by increasing the reward side. For example, we may ask for an increased salary, a better commission schedule, or a bonus in the form of money or privileges.

If we have success at neither of these balancing attempts, we may decide to wipe the board clean entirely by quitting. This action effectively takes us out of what we perceive as an inequitable comparison with others. We may also feel our resignation pays back those who caused the inequity; for a period of weeks or longer, they may have trouble filling our former spot. We imagine that they regret their inequitable actions.

Third, we can attempt to re-establish equitable balance between ourselves and others by changing their side of the equation. We could insist, for example, that the other person work harder or receive less money. Fourth, we can attempt to substitute another ratio for the one we dislike. Instead of comparing ourselves disadvantageously to Person A in the company, we may switch our perspective entirely and begin comparing ourselves to Person B.

In Peggy Woodward's case, for example, her company might decide to label the four hard-working managers as participants in the company's "fast track" program. The other two managers would not be considered fast-trackers. Although her salary, responsibilities, and raise have not changed a whit, Peggy is now content with the new arrangement; she compares herself only to the other three hard-working managers. That comparison, she feels, is equitable.

Finally, we can attempt to tilt the balance to the even point or toward our favor by psychologically distorting the data used for comparison. Peggy, for example, might take an empathetic view of one manager's child-care responsibilities or another's need for further education. This new perspective may make her feel more content with the apparent imbalance in work. Some theorists, however, argue that balance is still at issue: Peggy is saying to herself, in effect, that her own total pain for pay is less than or equal to another person's total pain for pay, when childcare or other matters are factored into the equation. In this version, Peggy just doesn't want anyone to have it easier than she does.

Another psychological distortion technique involves what Leon Festinger calls "cognitive dissonance." When our perceptions of the outer world support our perceptions of ourselves and our own interests, these perceptions are said to be in a consonant relationship. Peggy's perception of the three hard-working managers is consonant with her perception of her own role and value. But Peggy's perception of the idle managers is dissonant with her perception of herself. In other words, she cannot simultaneously believe that she is being treated equitably and they are being treated equitably.

One common response to cognitive dissonance, Festinger points out, is to quit hearing in part or in full. Peggy may select out only those aspects of an idle manager's work day that are consonant for her: "Well, she delegates well, and I guess that counts for something." Or Peggy may shut out all information from the dissonant source: "I don't want to hear about it. I get so angry. I just want to do my job and be left alone."

Or Peggy may respond to cognitive dissonance by practicing the psychological defense of disbelief. Festinger's research demonstrates that "heavy smokers are less likely to believe that there is a relationship between smoking and lung cancer than nonsmokers." In Peggy's case, she may choose not to believe what she hears about the idle managers. "I've heard the stories, but I'm sure they're not getting away with half of what people say. It's all gossip and it doesn't bother me one bit."

Finally, what about the "up" side of the equity equation? How do we respond when we discover ourselves to be overpaid or overprivileged in comparison to our equally hard-working peers? Research is mixed. On one hand, studies point to corporate superstars who give of themselves in direct proportion to their pay. "Because I earn $125,000 a year here," one vice president says, "I would be ashamed not to give the company at least a 60-hour week." On the other hand, there are studies of some tenured professors and other high pay/high security professionals that show a significant dip in productivity compared to their lower-pay/lower-security career periods.

But one fact stands out incontrovertibly for those interested in motivation: when people feel that they are the victims of inequity, they lose motivation to accomplish company goals. (Interestingly, they may not lose motivation *per se*. An employee angered by felt inequity may be highly motivated to complain, join or organize supportive groups, and even vandalize company property and projects.)

MANAGEMENT TIPS

Managers sometimes cause inequities by the way they distribute rewards. But just as often, as in the Peggy Woodward case, inequities develop as a result of worker actions. No matter what the cause, perceived inequities can be minimized in these ways:

1. Managers should study their organizations to determine where equity comparisons are likely to be made.
2. Managers can influence equity comparisons by distinguishing job titles, job descriptions, chains of reporting, numbers of employees supervised, and types of rewards distributed.
3. Managers can prevent some forms of equity comparison by restricting the information available to employees about amounts and types of rewards given to others.

4. Managers can reduce the negative impact of unavoidable inequities (as perceived) by the ethical use of expectation motivators. Employees who feel "cheated" in the short term may continue to work hard toward company goals if they have reasonable expectation of just rewards in the long term.

CHAPTER 4

WHAT DO YOU THINK ABOUT YOUR JOB?

Motivators and Your Work Attitudes

Key factors to employee motivation may lie primarily in the outside world.

Richard Young, 25, is a systems analyst for a Miami computer company. In that capacity, he accompanies sales people on their calls and offers technical advice on what hardware and software to buy for particular applications. Richard is engaged to be married within a year.

I have very strong opinions about my present job. Not that anyone in the company is listening. I expect to quit soon. If it weren't for the expenses of my upcoming marriage, I would probably be out the door already.

Here's what I face. This company is making money hand over fist, even in a slow economy. Everyone wants to upgrade their old XT personal computers to the new 286, 386, and 486 series. Making sales is like shooting fish in a barrel. I walk into a client's company with a salesperson who usually knows next to nothing about computers but is personable and attractive. He or she introduces me as a computer expert. The client describes the problem and I come up with the computer solution. Usually it's a true no-brainer. If the client needs more processing power, we sell a 386 or 486 machine. If the client needs more terminals, we sell a simple network to link PCs. I could do it in my sleep.

But getting back to my point: the company is getting rich on these easy sales. And what happens to those profits? In its infinite wisdom, the company's executive committee has decided to spend heavily on a "stimulating work environment" for employees. So in my office I have a $1000 walnut desk, three leather chairs, and some original, signed artwork on the wall. We have an expensive new "dining lounge" instead of the old coffee room. We're driving Lincolns as company cars instead of Chevrolets, and of course we each must have a car phone. Thanks to the executive committee, I'm now the proud owner of a benefits plan that will pay for anything, anytime, anywhere.

Don't get me wrong. These fringe advantages are nice, and friends nearly keel over when they walk into my luxurious office. But what do all these trappings have to do with my job?

What do I think about my job? I'll tell you the truth. I think the company is under-utilizing me. I'm paraded around like some kind of swami to utter a bit of techno-babble to sell a client on a few PCs. The company should be going after more challenging sales. I would love to get involved in more complicated computer situations for business or government. I'd like to go after big fish and get rewarded accordingly if I brought them in.

The company thinks it's making me happy by giving me thicker carpets and more flex-time. But the truth is that not even more money will keep me from looking elsewhere. I don't mind working hard when I'm using and building my skills. But I don't like treading water, even in the executive Jacuzzi.

FOLLOW-UP INFORMATION

Richard Young graduated with a B.S. in computer science from UCLA, with a GPA of 3.92. In his spare time, he experiments with new computer devices of his own invention. Richard keeps in touch with many of his college friends, many of whom are working in research positions for IBM, Xerox, and Apple. They rarely ask about his job but are always eager to hear about his experimenting. Richard's fiancee admires him for many qualities, especially his intelligence.

MOTIVATORS AT WORK

As early as 1924, researchers interested in work efficiency suspected that the key factors to employee motivation may lie primarily in the outside world, not within the individual worker. In that year, efficiency experts at Western Electric Company of Hawthorne, Illinois, began to study the effects of illumination upon work productivity.

Following usual scientific methods, they selected a test group of employees and a comparable control group. Lighting in the rooms occupied by the test group was gradually increased. As expected, the productivity of the test group rose as illumination increased.

But to the surprise of researchers, the productivity of the control group also rose—and without any change in their illumination.

These unusual results attracted the interest of Harvard's Elton Mayo. Over a period of two years, Mayo and his team tried all manner of workplace enhancements upon test groups—rest breaks, company-paid lunches, more comfortable work stations, and so forth. To their astonishment, control groups without these emoluments performed as well or better than the test groups. Finally, researchers took away all work enhancements from the test groups and plunged them back to their original work conditions. Surely, researchers thought, we will now see productivity plunge as well as workers react negatively to these changes.

Just the opposite occurred. Production for the test groups reached an all-time high.

From these famous experiments has come a term familiar to every social researcher: the Hawthorne effect. Mayo and his team had discovered in Hawthorne, Illinois, that *any* group singled out for special attention, even for control purposes, will usually respond by increased motivation. If only for a brief moment, these selected workers felt themselves to be on stage, in the spotlight. They performed accordingly.

It is ironic, in fact, that these early studies of the physical workplace should give rise to the human relations movement in business and industry. The Hawthorne researchers had demonstrated that *people* make the difference in organizations, seldom because of their surroundings and often in spite of them.

In the opening scenario of this chapter, Richard Young's company hasn't yet gotten the message implicit in the Hawthorne experiments. Richard's company is still trying to motivate him and other employees by creature comforts: nice offices, luxury cars, portable phones, and the rest.

These workplace enhancements, in the language made famous by Frederick Herzberg, are *maintenance factors*. (Herzberg also called them hygiene factors—conducive to good business health but not the cause of it.)

In studying the nature of work motivation, Herzberg and his colleagues began by interviewing accountants and engineers from various companies. These people were each asked two questions:

> "Tell me about a time when you felt exceptionally good about your job."
> "Tell me about a time when you felt exceptionally bad about your job."

After analyzing more than 4,000 responses to these questions Herzberg and his team saw a clear pattern present. When people wanted to express satisfaction with their jobs, they listed a predictable list of things they like. Herzberg called these "satisfiers" or motivators. But when it came to expressing dissatisfaction with their jobs, people did not list the absence of satisfiers, as might be expected. Instead, they came up with a separate list Herzberg was to call "dissatisfiers" or maintenance factors.

Here, first, are the top six satisfiers identified by Herzberg's study:

- Achievement
- Recognition
- The work itself
- Responsibility
- Advancement
- Growth

By contrast, here are the top six dissatisfiers from the same study:

- Company policy and administration
- Supervision
- Relationship with supervisor
- Work conditions
- Relationships with peers
- Relationships with subordinates

In complaining about company policies and administration, interviewees pointed to missing or unfair grievance procedures, poor performance appraisal methods, rigid attendance rules, and impractical vacation schedules. Typical complaints about work conditions included safety hazards, claustrophobia in confined space, lack of personal comfort at work stations, noise levels, and air pollutants.

But solve any one of these maintenance factors and what do you have? A motivated employee? Not at all. Herzberg's point is that what it takes to satisfy an employee's needs (i.e., motivate him or her) differs from what it takes to maintain a complaint-free or even praiseworthy work environment.

Put another way, a lousy work environment can lower motivation, but a superb work environment alone can't create it.

Let's consider Richard Young in relation to his company. Richard understands clearly what he wants from his company, and his "wish list" accords closely with Herzberg's satisfiers. Richard wants to achieve to his capacity, not tread water even for attractive pay. He wants to extend his knowledge and skill through challenging work experiences. He wants recognition, perhaps most of all from his college computer buddies, for his own professional work in the field. He wants to enjoy the stimulation of the work itself; the computer field has apparently fascinated him for many years.

But instead of listening to Richard's list of satisfiers, his company has wrong-headedly decided to eliminate any potential dissatisfiers. Probably without knowing anything about Herzberg's studies, the company nonetheless marched down the list of typical dissatisfiers in their efforts to motivate Richard. Company policies were loosened to the point of *laissez faire*; supervision was only on an as-needed basis; work conditions were glamorized by expensive offices and cars; and worker relations were similarly spiced by frequent office parties, social gatherings, and get-away vacation prizes for employees.

But so what? Richard's eagerness to find other employment is eloquent testimony to the crucial differences between motivators (satisfiers) and maintenance factors.

Do We All Have the Same Motivators?

Periodically throughout the 1980s, management experts Paul Hersey and Kenneth H. Blanchard have replicated a study first published in 1949 by Lawrence Lindahl. He set out to determine whether supervisors are motivated by the same things that motivate rank-and-file workers. The relative positions of importance assigned to ten motivators by supervisors and workers are shown on the following page.

The results in our day, report Hersey and Blanchard, have not changed substantially for managers. "The only

	Supervisors' Ranking	Workers' Ranking
Good working conditions	4	9
Feeling "in" on things	10	2
Tactful disciplining	7	10
Appreciation for work done	8	1
Management loyalty to workers	6	8
Good wages	1	5
Promotion and growth with company	3	7
Understanding of personal problems	9	3
Job security	2	4
Interesting work	5	6

Priority of Wanted Job Aspects (1 = highest)

real changes," they write, "seem to be that workers, over the last five to ten years, were increasing in their desire for 'promotion and growth with the company' and 'interesting work'." And, Hersey and Blanchard point out, in times of economic decline, workers again emphasize "good wages" and "job security."

The implications of these studies are important for both supervisors and workers. If you're a supervisor or manager, you may select motivators for your workers based on your own list of high-priority motivators. Because a 10 percent raise (your item #1) would send you over the moon with joy, you might assume that a 10 percent raise will prove similarly motivating to your entry level employees. But consider that "good wages" was no more than number 5 on their list of wants. Understandably, entry level workers raised from $4.10 per hour to $4.41 (a 10 percent raise) may not be instantly motivated to work like John Henry. A few, in fact, may yawn.

MANAGEMENT TIPS

A clear understanding of the differences between motivators and maintenance factors helps managers select motivators that connect with worker needs.

1. In assessing motivational programs, managers should watch for the Hawthorne Effect. Any employee or group of employees highlighted for special attention will respond with temporarily increased productivity.

2. Dissatisfying work conditions can restrict the capacity of workers to perform and their motivation to do so.

3. The elimination of dissatisfying work factors does not automatically create a satisfying and motivating work climate.

4. Motivators (satisfiers) may be different for each individual. Managers have to understand an individual worker's wants in order to choose effective motivators.

5. Managers often have a set of motivators different in priority from those of workers. Managers should not impose their motivator priorities on others who do not share those priorities.

CHAPTER 5

WHAT DOES THE BOSS THINK OF YOU?

Motivators and Approval

What your employer thinks about you can be a powerful motivational influence, for better or for worse.

Linda Perelli, 26, has worked as a buyer for a chain of suburban Los Angeles clothing stores for four years. She is married with two children.

I'll tell you what I've experienced at this company and what I know others have experienced. It's not a gender thing or a matter of race. But it's prejudice nonetheless.

Two brothers own this company. Both are in their late 50s and they spend all day, every day, supervising us in the office. That's Supervise with a capital S.

These bosses make it obvious what they think of their employees. In their eyes, we're all lazy or mischievous children that have to be watched, scolded, and nagged throughout the day. One or the other of them literally stands by the entrance door at 9:00 a.m. every morning to see who's exactly on time and who's a minute or two late. Believe me, if you're one of the unlucky people who comes in at 9:05 or 9:10, you're going to get a very surly memo the next day. Lunches and breaks are the same story.

I've worked in other companies, and I can assure

you that these two bosses have nothing to complain about with their workers. Almost without exception, everyone here tries to do a good job and go the extra mile—but in spite of, not because of, the behavior of the bosses. We do have a lot of turnover, however. About every six weeks, someone seems to "get into it" with one of the two brothers, and then there's another empty desk.

My husband and I often talk about why these two men act this way. I don't think they enjoy their work at all anymore, so they assume that their employees hate work as well. Their only feeble attempt at motivating us is the repeated promise of some kind of bonus if we can exceed our sales goals. In my four years here, I have seen only two yearly bonuses, both of them less than $3,000.

Let me give you two typical examples of what we're up against. Because of sudden resignations, a senior management slot opened up a month ago. We in the office had to read about the opening in the newspaper; the two brothers assumed that no one already on staff was bright enough or ambitious enough to be interested in the job.

Then there are our irregular staff meetings. The two brothers chair the meeting and basically lecture us for two hours on how expenses are going up, shoplifters are everywhere, and we're not earning our salaries. Sometimes they open up a topic for discussion, but we've all learned never to suggest solutions to problems. The brothers consider themselves the only ones capable of solutions. Our job in discussion is just to fill out the details about the problem itself.

Why do I stay? It's close to home, I have some seniority here, and my husband works in the same building. Would I like a better job, even at less salary? You bet . . . and I'm looking.

FOLLOW-UP INFORMATION

Eight years ago, the two brothers who own Linda's company were victims of an elaborate embezzlement scheme by several key employees, some of whom the brothers had befriended. Their losses were never recovered, nor was their trust in employees. But no matter what the brothers' reasons for their management style, Linda feels stalled in her own development as a buyer. "I never get a chance to try my ideas," she complains.

MOTIVATORS IN ACTION

Imagine yourself a factory superintendent some two hundred years ago during the first stages of the Industrial Revolution in England. You arrive at work to face a horde of laborers, most of them recently driven into the city by government agricultural "reforms." These men, women, and children are generally ill-fed, ill-clothed, and ill-housed. They are ready to do virtually anything for a day's meager pay. But they have no skills. Few can even read. If given the chance, some will steal in their desperation.

How do you manage your "workforce"? Elizabeth Gaskell describes the bleak beginnings of factory life in her novel, *North and South*. Later, Charles Dickens traces the sad social results of that system in *Hard Times*. Both novelists make clear how these workers were managed: like animals.

The more polite term by the turn of our century had become the Rabble Hypothesis. The laboring masses were often viewed by industrialists and finance barons as virtual beasts of burden, to be driven by the whips of fear and held captive to employment by financial chokehold. Managers were advised to rule with an iron fist: Drive up production by threatening workers with punishment and termination. Banish "trouble-makers" from employment at the first hint of objection. Hire and fire on the spot to match the ups and downs of business.

The human reaction eventually challenged such treatment, and immortal descriptions of that process lie at the heart of works like *The Grapes of Wrath* and *The Jungle*. But the Rabble Hypothesis did not disappear for managers.

According to Douglas McGregor, the rigid attitudes of many nineteenth century managers were simply rephrased into new language for the twentieth century. McGregor terms this new version of the Rabble Hypothesis the "Theory X" theory of management.

Notice in its tenets (as listed on the next page), however, the remaining pessimism about human nature and motivation.

This is the work environment that appalls Linda Perelli. She no doubt believes quite different things about herself in relation to her work. Yet in frustration she also feels herself becoming in part the bitter, vindictive, and uncommitted employee her bosses treat her as.

For much of his career, social scientist Chris Argyris focused on this management problem. In his view, many organizations are designed according to principles and assumptions that keep immature people from developing to their potential and, just as often, cause mature people like Linda Perelli to become less mature. McGregor, Argyris, Hersey, Blanchard, and other management researchers agree that most business organizations in the United States continue to be run according to Theory X principles.

Argyris's strongest argument against such management of human beings springs from his succinct description of human developmental stages. Left to our natural development from infancy to adulthood, he says, we human beings move from:

- passivity to activity
- dependence to independence
- limited behaviors to complex behaviors
- flighty interests to profound interests

Theory X Management Assumptions

1. Most people hate work.

2. Most people want to avoid responsibility.

3. Most people have little ambition for themselves.

4. Most people prefer to be led.

5. Most people have little ability to solve problems.

6. Most people are motivated to work primarily for food, shelter, clothing, and security.

7. Most people require close control to prevent mistakes and prohibit loafing.

- "now" thinking to past, present, and future perspectives
- subordinance to equality and leadership
- lack of self awareness to selfhood and self control

But too many organizations, Argyris finds, try to move us *backward* along this natural developmental path. Workers are often encouraged to be passive and accepting, to follow the leader unthinkingly, to restrict their attention to trivial problems, to leave long range planning to the bosses, to accept perpetual subordination as their lot, and to put little stock in one's self (a replaceable cog within the company machine).

Managers in these organizations, concludes Argyris, have no room to complain if their workers seem unmotivated and unresourceful. The very management structure of the company has created such slaves. Along the way, strong and independent selves like Linda Perelli probably left the company in droves. Just as Linda contemplates leaving her present employment, these talented workers feared eventually becoming the drones they were assumed to be by management. For both McGregor and Argyris, the alternative to "Theory X" management involves a liberalized view of human nature and motivation. In his description of "Theory Y" assumptions, McGregor looks toward a new generation of managers and new assumptions.

People treated by these assumptions will act according to them—and the organization will be the primary beneficiary. Linda Perelli, for example, would love to work in an environment where her creativity and ambition (both for herself and her company) could take wing. In such an environment, it would be natural for Linda to stay late to finish up a stimulating project. The old factory concept of arriving "on time" or staying "over-time" in fact, would give way to more flexible ideas of work scheduling.

Are any companies actually run according to Theory Y assumptions in 1991? Emphatically yes. The general rule is holding more and more true that all companies in

Theory Y Management Assumptions

1. Work can be as enjoyable as play.

2. Most people want to accept reasonable levels of responsibility.

3. Most people have strong goals for themselves, and seek organizations that will help them fulfill those goals.

4. Most people like to lead occasionally.

5. Most people are good problem-solvers.

6. Most people in a prosperous society are motivated by goals beyond the physiological and security levels.

7. Most people require no policing or close control by the organization.

a seller's market for employees (a time when companies can't find all the talent they need) must employ at least some Theory Y principles to keep their workforce. No self-motivated adult, after all, willingly endures the kind of treatment the two brothers are dispensing on Linda and her co-workers. Examples of current companies with strong Theory Y management commitments are Apple Computer, IBM, Johnson & Johnson, Price-Waterhouse, TRW, and many others.

In summary, what your employer thinks about you can be a powerful motivational influence, for better or for worse. The boss's assumptions about you are evidenced especially by:

- where you are placed in the company structure. Are you a co-equal member of a team (Theory Y) or a subordinate in a strict reporting order (Theory X)?
- how you receive work instructions. Are you involved as a participant in problem-solving and task development (Theory Y) or are you told precisely what you are to do and when (Theory X)?
- how you are urged to organize your time. Can you allocate your time according to your own work progress (Theory Y) or are you told how much time you must give to particular tasks (Theory X)?
- how you relate to other levels of decision-making in the company. Can you speak freely about ideas and concerns to any level of management (Theory Y) or must you always "go through channels" (Theory X)?
- how you perceive your work tasks in relation to the larger business mission of the company. Do you understand what your individual work contributes to the whole (Theory Y) or do you work largely in a knowledge vacuum, without much idea of the value of your contribution (Theory X)?

As a footnote, it must be said that even in the most liberal Theory Y organizations the principles and techniques of Theory X management are occasionally employed. An uncommitted, immature employee may sometimes need to be told explicitly what to do and when. But even in such cases, the continued application of Theory X principles will not lead to the result the employer wants: a mature, contributing employee. For that result in the long term, the assumptions of Theory Y management are indispensable.

MANAGEMENT TIPS

Theory X and Theory Y management techniques suggest very different motivational behaviors for managers. Theory Y managers:

1. ask employees what they think about business problems.
2. encourage group discussion and evaluation.
3. welcome tentative judgments and speculative ideas.
4. thank employees for their efforts.
5. trust employees to work toward company goals.
6. free employees to develop individual skills for use within the company.
7. involve employees in the fair evaluation of their work.

For some, this description of work life may seem hopelessly Pollyannish. Yet, like Linda Perelli, we each probably feel that *we* could thrive in such a work climate. If we would choose a Theory Y management environment for ourselves, should we consider it too idealistic for others? That kind of double standard would bring us full circle back to the Rabble Hypothesis.

CHAPTER 6

WHAT DO YOUR CO-WORKERS THINK OF YOU?

Motivators and Your Reputation

The power and actions of a group can be explained by examining its components.

John Fields, 29, is a deed specialist with a large New England title company. He is single.

Without bragging, I would describe myself as very popular among my co-workers, by which I mean the sixteen or so people who check on deeds and title chains all day. It's not exactly fascinating work, so we have this elaborate social stuff that goes on all day. It's mostly a matter of funny comments to each other and occasional practical jokes on someone. But it makes the day pass faster.

Most of us have been here at least three years, so we've been through a lot together: stolen cars, breakups in the relationships, money problems, and the rest. But it's brought us all closer. I feel that some of my most loyal friends are the people I work with every day.

It's almost humorous at times how close we are. Last month the company hired for our group a guy we quickly came to call "the nerd"—absolutely no sense of humor, a real loner. We didn't do anything to make life hard for him, but it was obvious that he just didn't fit in. Within a couple of weeks he had quit. One of my friends here put it well: "If you don't click, you gotta quit!"

*Another advantage of our closeness as a group is
the whole matter of raises. The company is on a merit
system, which in itself is absurd. How can you
measure whether one employee is really working
harder or better than another? I might have more
difficult cases that just take longer to process. Should
I be penalized for being thorough?*

*Anyway, our group has resisted the unfairness of
the merit system by informally agreeing on how many
files we'll each process during the day. Our division
manager knows that we have this limit, and doesn't
try to push us beyond it. I'd like to see her try.*

*This was one aspect of work life that college
didn't prepare me for. A lot of days I feel like I'm
back in the frat house—all for one and one for all.*

FOLLOW-UP INFORMATION

In actual fact, John Fields is among the least popular members of his work group. Behind his back, co-workers often mock his constant efforts to find playmates at work. John's superiors rank him as doubtful for promotion. They are particularly concerned about his inability to complete assignments on time and his misuse of work time for social relations.

MOTIVATORS AT WORK

S. E. Asch conducted a memorable experiment that demonstrated the power of groups to motivate individual behavior. He placed a line on a display board. Beside it were three other lines, only one of which was the same length as the line set off by itself. Then Asch brought in groups of eight college men. Each student was asked in turn which of the three lines was the same length as the isolated line. Secretly, Asch had instructed seven of the eight students to give the same wrong answer. He wanted to discover how strong the influence of the group would be on the uninitiated eighth member. Would he report what

A. _____

_____ B. _____

C. _____

The Asch Experiment: Which line matches the original in length?

he saw to be true or would he go along with the obviously incorrect, but unanimous, answer of the rest of the group?

Asch discovered that "one-third of all the estimates were errors identical with or in the direction of the distorted estimates of the majority."

This tendency of group members to lose their individual evaluative abilities is called "Groupthink" by social psychologist Irving Janis. Groups that want or need to be highly cohesive resist original thoughts and actions that may lead to disharmony or jealousy in the group. The result is often inaction or poor decision-making by group members. No one member wants to stand out for honor or for blame; to do so risks banishment from the group.

Most of the primary symptoms of Groupthink are probably present in John Fields' office. John Fields has many reasons, both conscious and unconscious, for wanting to be a secure member of his work group. As one of the less competent employees, he needs the protection of the group to shield him from the potential actions of management. If I'm "in" with the group, John reasons, the boss won't criticize me for fear of having a lot of people upset with him. In these thoughts, John is projecting onto the boss his own belief in the power of the group.

John also needs steady approval from the group. In the language of Alfred Adler, he *compensates* for his deep feelings of unworthiness and social unattractiveness by trying, ironically, to be the most sociable person in the office. He seeks the hour-by-hour approval of the group to assuage his painful feelings aroused by an *inferiority complex*. John therefore turns almost every work interaction into an occasion for getting praise, approval, or just attention.

The group, however, has already begun to banish John, though so far without his knowledge. Why push out someone with such strong desires to be friendly? The group recognizes that John is self-seeking in his interactions; he wants something *from* the group, but not *for* the

GROUPTHINK MAY BE STRONG WHEN MEMBERS BELIEVE . . .

- "No one can resist the will of the group."

- "Data in conflict with group information must be incorrect."

- "The group wouldn't do the wrong thing morally."

- "Nongroup competitors are stupid and weak."

- "All group members should wholeheartedly support one position."

- "If you do have private reservations, it's best to keep your mouth shut."

- "There's probably no need to discuss topics, since the group will quickly agree."

- "Information conflicting with group positions isn't worth hearing."

group. To that extent, he's quickly identified as a non-contributor to group welfare and potentially dangerous to the interests of the group.

What will be John's fate in the company? Management already seems to have identified him for the slow track—the one that leads out the door. As John begins to receive negative signals from management, he will no doubt carry them directly to the group: "You wouldn't believe what the manager put on my performance evaluation." Directly or indirectly, group members will communicate to John that they won't rally to his cause; in effect, he will learn where he really stands with the group. At this point, John will probably quit to seek a new and, he hopes, more supportive group with another company. John will no doubt explain to his new employer that "I got along great with my co-workers, but the manager just didn't like me. I don't know why. It was a personality conflict, I guess."

HOW GROUPS WORK

George C. Homans describes groups in terms of three interrelated elements:

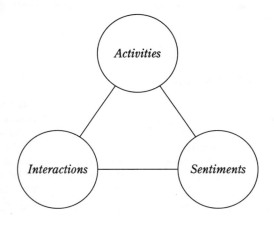

All workers in the group perform activities of some sort—writing reports, designing layouts, building products, and so forth. To accomplish these activities, workers must interact. And in the process of that interaction, workers develop a shared set of sentiments. Homans' central point is that a change in any one of these elements influences the other elements. In other words, the power and actions of the group can be explained by examining its component elements.

Let's say, for example, that the group develops strongly negative sentiments about salaries paid by the company. The interactions immediately change in character; group members begin to meet less for business purposes and more to share opinions and information about the pay problem. Activities slow dramatically as worker motivation falls off.

Or consider the spiraling effect that often leads to highly cohesive groups. In their initial interactions, workers find that they enjoy each other's company. Sentiments begin to warm. The change in this element encourages even more interaction—which in turn increases sentiments. All the while, activities may show little increase and may actually decrease. It's possible, in other words, to have a highly social workplace where little actual work gets done.

Managing the Motivation of Groups

Almost by definition, managers are excluded from the tight bonds and trust of the group. No matter how politely the manager is treated by group members, he or she remains the primary threat to the cohesion of the group. The manager, after all, is the one who can physically separate the group by reassignment, destroy group unity by promotions and demotions, disturb group habits by new tasks, and disrupt group membership by hiring and firing. From the group's point of view, the manager is the potential enemy.

The manager usually has full knowledge of the group's overt activities—the production line and work flow are easily observed. But the manager may know little about the group's private interactions and true sentiments. This information is carried by an informal but powerful channel of communication called the grapevine. In a 1984 survey of 10,000 employees, respondents were asked, "What are your major current sources of organizational information?" When asked to answer that question by choosing from fifteen categories, employees listed "immediate supervisor" first and "the grapevine" second.

Some managers (acting in response to cognitive dissonance, described in Chapter 3) do whatever they can to "tune out" the grapevine. They want to live with the illusion that workers are relatively contented, that the opinions of management are law, and that it's business as usual. These managers make sure their offices are located far from the action of the workplace. They keep their doors closed. They hire secretaries who won't share what they hear over coffee. They eat with other managers, never with workers. In short, they believe that "what I don't know can't hurt me."

Unfortunately, these are usually the same managers who have no explanation when production schedules fall behind or key workers quit.

Other managers try to listen to the rumblings carried by the grapevine. They cannot, of course, hear everything shared by bona fide group members. Instead, the manager uses informal occasions during lunches and breaks, and before and after meetings to listen. When the group senses that the manager is interested in the grapevine in a nonthreatening way, the group often finds subtle ways of sharing particularly important rumors, questions, or concerns with the manager. Two or three group members may "have the manager's ear" without sacrificing their secure standing within the group.

MANAGEMENT TIPS

Groups exert powerful influence over the thoughts, feelings, and actions of group members. To harness some of the positive power of groups, managers should:

1. Listen to the grapevine, especially when it carries distressing news.
2. Counteract false rumors and incorrect information heard via the grapevine. The manager can use formal channels of communication—the company newsletter, memos, and meetings—to clarify facts and reduce apprehensions.
3. Structure group assignments and interactions to reduce the negative influence of power cliques.

CHAPTER 7

WHAT DO YOU THINK OF YOURSELF?

Motivators and Your Self-Image

We are each the sum total of our life habits.

Helen Pulaski, 57, is publications assistant for a Detroit company that manufactures automobile seats. Her primary responsibility is to help produce a monthly newsletter and various company brochures. She lives alone with two cats.

> *I don't often think of myself at all. I've had this job so long that I can't even find my resume anymore. If you asked people that I work with, I think they would describe me as punctual and competent. I know the English language well and very few errors having to do with grammar, punctuation, or spelling ever creep into my work.*
>
> *I have pleasant working relations with others in the office. I'm often asked about my cats. I keep a file of office birthdays and send out cards when they occur. I've done this for years for everyone from the president to the janitor. I think people appreciate it.*
>
> *As for my work life, there are no problems as far as I know. The newsletter hasn't received any complaints. My work has become easier since the managers send me minutes of their meetings instead of having me attend. I can retire at 60, and I plan to work full-steam up to that point.*

I would describe myself as settled and comfortable. I have very few ups or downs, just life as usual each day. In the office, I've maintained some traditional practices, such as using my Underwood typewriter instead of a computer. I get teased every once in a while about this, but everyone in the office knows that it's just my way. I get my work done, and that's what matters. If it takes me longer, I just stay later. It's my choice.

FOLLOW-UP INFORMATION

Helen Pulaski grew up as the only daughter of a Presbyterian minister and his wife. Helen was praised for keeping her room neat and punished for rough play. At 17, Helen became pregnant and gave birth to a baby boy in an out-of-state church facility. At her father's insistence, the baby was privately put out for adoption. Helen returned to her parent's home, where she lived until their deaths a decade later. Helen then took work as a secretary and gradually worked her way into her present position in publications. Helen likes regular schedules and repetitive tasks. She says that she cannot function at all during rush jobs and unexpected company crises. Her co-workers think she's right.

MOTIVATORS AT WORK

What to do about Helen . . . That's every manager's problem, for most larger offices have their Helens and Herberts: decent people with long service to the company but little usefulness.

Helen's basic problem, of course, is that she is Helen. Co-workers say as much: "That's just Helen—not much you can do." In motivating Helen to new levels of achievement (or even previous levels of achievement), we first have to figure out how Helen became Helen.

THE PROCESS OF PERSONALITY FORMATION

We are each the sum total of our life habits. Helen's personality, for example, is the result of 57 years of her own experimentation and evaluation. As a very young child, Helen may have experimented vocally by shouting or screaming. Her mother and father punished her. Helen learned not to shout or scream. She probably went on to experiment with ways of playing, ways of expressing anger, ways of showing joy. In each case, her parents and teachers were significant forces in shaping Helen's eventual habits. Yes, Helen. No, Helen. Go to your room, Helen.

Without dragging Freud from his grave, it's probably safe to say that Helen's last important experiment in personal freedom involved the love affair that led to her pregnancy at 17. Her parents would not allow her to marry the young man or keep the baby. The whole matter was guarded within the family circle as a shameful tragedy for which Helen was to blame. Helen spent her twenties caring for her aging parents—paying them, in effect, for their "kindness" to her during her pregnancy and its emotional aftermath.

The Helen that sits before us now at 57 is the sum total of a life dedicated to self-doubt, self-denial, apology, and safety. She has learned in a thousand ways over the years that routine is good, that emergencies are bad; that simple tasks are comfortable, that complex tasks are painful; that boredom is sanity, that excitement breeds disappointment.

MOTIVATING RESTRICTED PERSONALITIES

Some managers give up on the Helens in the office. Staff reductions are engineered in a way that cuts out their job descriptions. Transfers or early retirements are urged upon them, with the manager's reassurance that "it's best for you."

Fortunately, other managers refuse to push out people who know company operations and have given years of their lives to company interests. Against all odds, these managers cherish the belief that Helen, even in her later years, can be motivated to succeed at new challenges. These are the managers who believe in "personality renaissance"—that our limitations (our "mind-forged manacles," in the poet Blake's phrase) are self-imposed and self-controlled. We can undo what we've done to ourselves.

Thomas Harris, M.D., calls Helen's view of herself in relation to others her "life position." From an early age, Helen has come to think of herself as essentially "not OK"—she disobeyed Mom and Dad, she had an illegitimate child, and on and on. Other people, in Helen's view, are generally "OK." They seem so brave, so eager, so confident. In this "I'm not OK, you're OK" life position, Helen is more than content to perform the most routine, dreary tasks; she actually looks forward to stuffing envelopes and filing correspondence. In such simple tasks she runs no risk of having her not-OK status confirmed once again. The new and exciting tasks in the office can be left, she feels, for all those people who are OK.

Employees can assume any one of four life positions. Ideally, a co-worker feels "I'm OK, you're OK. We are both secure enough to take on work challenges without fearing a devastating loss in self-esteem." Conversely, an employee can feel "I'm not OK, you're not OK." These are the people who despair not only for themselves but for the universe: "We have no chance for success. Let's just give up." Or a person can feel "I'm OK, you're not OK." These are the egotists who always know better, or believe they do. Interestingly, these types use night as a way of defining day, so to speak. They rise above the rest of us in their own view by putting us down. And, as we have seen in Helen's case, there are those who feel "I'm not OK, you're OK."

Each of our life positions can vary somewhat from day to day. But one position recurs more than any other, and it is this dominant position that defines our view of ourselves and way of relating to others.

What's a manager to do with an office full of "I'm not-OKs" or "you're not-OKs"? Some companies are fortunate to have counselling services available for particularly distressed personalities. But surely the hard work of psychological therapy is beyond the manager's job description and expertise. No manager can undo all of the effects of Helen's childhood and adolescence. Yet a manager must act in some way, especially when company goals are going unmet because of personality problems among the workers.

Perhaps the best option for managers is to take a chance and promote "OKness" among all employees. As Dr. Harris relates from his own practice, even the glimpse of "possible OKness" can spread like wildfire within the individual personality and eventually within the workplace.

Let's apply a healthy dose of "OKness" to Helen's case and monitor the result. Helen, as we have seen, doesn't want to learn word-processing; she feels within that she will be setting herself up for another failure. She worries that "so many people in the office already know word-processing—I'll never catch up." But enter "OKness" in the form of her good-natured boss. Instead of asking her to learn all of word-processing, he simplifies the task to creating an address list on the computer. He chooses one of Helen's office friends to teach Helen what she needs to know for this task. The friend praises Helen often for her successes and makes light of failures. Gradually, Helen masters the skills involved in creating an address list. She expresses amazement at how much time the computer saves her in preparing and revising mailing labels.

From this simple beginning, Helen's personal renaissance begins. She learns other word-processing skills at home (her least threatening environment) and receives steady praise from her boss for the new skills she brings to the office. In time, people are commenting about "the new Helen," and relating to her in more positive ways. Her productivity and usefulness to the company increase dramatically.

MANAGEMENT TIPS

Although managers cannot play the role of therapist to their employees, they can motivate improved performance in at least eight ways:

1. Treat employees as "OK" individuals.

2. Focus on the actions, not the person, when delivering negative evaluations.

3. Emphasize high hopes for each employee's professional growth.

4. Make development opportunities such as training seminars available to employees.

5. Promote team consciousness and resist scapegoating.

6. Praise employees for efforts and achievements.

7. Reward employees fairly.

8. Forgive and forget when these responses will contribute to employee development and company success.

A FINAL NOTE

Perhaps as a carryover from the American "just-take-a-pill" approach to physical ills, we may be tempted to think that an employee's psychological distress can be "fixed" by a single, heart-to-heart conversation or a visit or two to a company counsellor.

Would that it were so. In reality, a manager has to prepare for a long undertaking in helping an employee clear away psychological obstacles to job performance. The success of that enterprise will be measured in small steps of improvement, not overnight transformation.

CHAPTER 8

WHAT ARE YOUR GOALS?

*Motivators and
Your Targets*

The actual process of developing work objectives begins at the highest organizational levels and then filters down.

R oger Ellison, 37, works as an engineer for a St. Louis aerospace contractor. He is married with three children.

I wish they would give me just one week to run this company. I would make one major change that would save thousands of hours of wasted labor and millions of dollars.

I would just tell everyone what to do.

It's just that simple (although my wife says my idea would only appeal to other engineers). Everywhere in this company, about half of the workers know what needs to be done on projects and the other half don't. The uninformed sit at their desks inventing "work" that makes no difference to anyone. Everyone appears to be working, of course.

An aerospace project—a new shuttle engine, let's say—is a massive undertaking involving hundreds of scientists, designers, engineers, technicians, and others. To keep from looking bad, these people will all busy themselves somehow during the work day; no one will go up to the boss and complain about nothing to do.

But I guarantee you that at least half of these workers couldn't explain to you at a given moment exactly what they were trying to accomplish and how it served the larger interest of the project and the company. Many are doing activities or pursuing research for the sake of reports, which are filed with a manager and passed along to the company library. Paychecks arrive and that's that.

But a lot of workers yearn for more order and participation in their careers. I'd love a boss just once to say to all of us in my work unit, "Look, here's what the company is trying to accomplish. I'm going to give each of you a piece of the project and explain how it contributes to the company's goal. Then I'll hold you each accountable for your piece in the puzzle. The company is counting on you to do your part."

What we usually get, however, is something much more vague. You don't find out exactly what you were supposed to be doing until annual evaluations, when the boss blames you for not doing it. It comes down to "Why didn't you tell me?" "But I did tell you!" and on and on.

There would be a lot less frustration around here if each of us knew at the beginning of each day what we were supposed to accomplish that day. If we get it done well, we're on track for a raise or promotion. If we blow it, we get retrained or eventually fired. It's logical and it's fair. Why isn't it happening?

FOLLOW-UP

In the fourteen years he has worked as an engineer, Roger Ellison has undergone that same number of year-end performance evaluations. In nine of those evaluations, Roger has scored high in relation to his peers. He knows, however, that these "evaluations" have rarely been based on objective evidence of his work effectiveness. Like many employees, Roger has perfected the art of corporate appearances. He understands the behaviors that will mark him as a "team player" and "valuable contributor." Roger doesn't consider himself any more phony than his co-workers. He considers himself a skilled engineer. But he does realize that his company has no meaningful way of defining tasks and measuring employee effectiveness. The *de facto* system within the company involves strategic friendships with management, name association with successful projects, and avoidance of high-risk assignments. Roger Ellison has learned to play the game well, but doesn't like it.

MOTIVATORS AT WORK

Like many talented employees, Roger Ellison wants to be *managed by objectives*. That concept, usually abbreviated as MBO, was introduced in America by Peter Drucker in the early 1950s and popularized world-wide by George Odiorne, John Humble, and others. In the 1980s, the MBO approach gained renewed attention through the publication of bestselling books such as *The One-Minute Manager* and *In Search of Excellence*. By the early 1990s, management by objectives has become the dominant management style in hundreds of major corporations, including Purex, Tenneco, and Black & Decker.

At heart, MBO involves joint goal-setting between a superior and a subordinate. The manager or supervisor wants to distribute necessary work in such a way that employees are challenged to use their individual skills without feeling overwhelmed or underutilized. The employees, similarly, want to negotiate an agreed-upon set of goals at which they can succeed, with reasonable effort.

Once clear goals have been established, the exact specification of tasks is often left to the employee, subject to managerial review. If the goal, for example, is the development of a site plan for a building, the company architect accepting that goal will not be told point-for-point how to go about developing the site plan. The architect's expertise is taken for granted.

Specific goals for various work units within a company must be arranged to fulfill general corporate goals. Although a manager may have substantial flexibility in determining which employee takes on particular goals, the manager usually does not have the option to alter or dismiss the major goals themselves. MBO negotiations, therefore, begin with the assumption that "someone in our group has to work toward this particular goal; the question is who's best for it."

When goals have been negotiated, they become the primary standard by which employee effectiveness is measured. In our earlier example, a company architect working toward the goal of developing a site plan agrees to produce approved renderings of that plan by a certain date. If that goal is accomplished on or before the deadline, the architect deserves company rewards (typically in the form of raises and promotion). If not, the architect may be in line for a variety of company demerits, including salary reduction or demotion.

MBO evaluation procedures, significantly, are behavior-based, not personality-based. When the company architect comes up for review, it is with the assurance that the performance evaluation won't be determined by such vague standards as "attitude toward work," "cooperation with others," and "interpersonal effectiveness." Instead, work performance will be primarily judged by one clear standard: were the agreed-upon goals met?

The actual process of developing work objectives begins at the highest organizational levels and then filters down to lower and lower levels in the organizational hierarchy. Because the process is cyclic in nature rather than linear, any significant change in specific goals at lower levels can eventually affect the re-definition of general goals at the highest organizational levels. In other words, the CEO may be driving the bus, but relying upon all the passengers to watch out for danger or better routes.

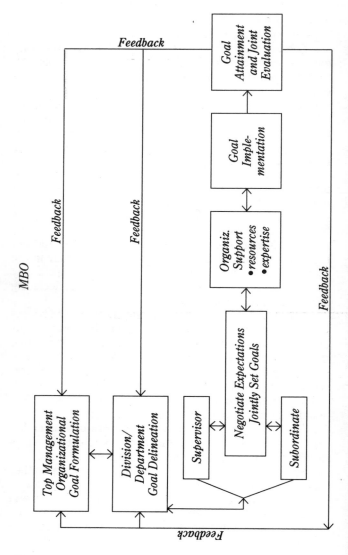

Management by objectives tends to fulfill employees' esteem and self-actualization needs (as explained in Chapter 1). Roger Ellison, in our opening scenario, isn't coming to work just to pick up a paycheck. He wants to apply his intelligence and training to interesting problems. As an expert in his field, he doesn't want a company executive to try to tell him precisely how to solve those problems. The executive, after all, probably knows much less than Roger about the matter. Roger wants to help determine clear goals, then be trusted to work out expert solutions. That trust on the part of the company breeds self-esteem and fulfillment for Roger. He feels loyal to his company because "I'm valued there."

NEGOTIATING PERFORMANCE OBJECTIVES

Much is at stake when a manager and a subordinate sit down to negotiate work goals. The manager's own success depends upon distributing work goals clearly, fairly, and appropriately. The employee, too, faces risks: the goals accepted will be the standard by which later performance is evaluated. As one employee quipped to a manager, "you're asking me to pick the rope you'll later use to hang me."

The effective negotiation of work goals, therefore, usually takes time and involves five key points:

The goal itself: What does the company want done?

The goal qualification: By what deadline must the goal be completed? Within what limits of quality control, inspection, or approval?

The available resources: What is the budget for achieving the goal? What personnel are available? What facilities, equipment, and supplies?

The standards of measurement: How will performance be measured? How often? By whom? How will measurement results be communicated?

What rewards are associated with successful performance?

The relative importance of the goal: What is at stake with regard to the goal? What visibility, risk, or responsibility comes with the goal?

Discussion of performance objectives usually focusses on all of these key issues. Some are more difficult to deal with than others, both for the manager and the subordinate. A salaried employee, for example, may opt for easier work goals if there's no incentive to accept more challenging assignments. In addition, the fear of failure for an employee may loom large for high-visibility, high-risk goals. Even when potential payoffs are great, many employees tend to "play it safe" rather than risk the embarrassment of failure and company notoriety.

In negotiating performance objectives, therefore, a manager must present work goals in such a way that they seem not just financially or intellectually attractive but also organizationally safe. Especially when considering high-risk goals, an employee has a right to know "what happens if I fail?" The manager who has a reasonable answer to that question can often win employee commitment to risky work tasks.

As MBO programs have sprung up across industries, management researchers have been eager to learn how well this approach to employee motivation works. In general, MBO systems score high marks both from top management and employees. At Cypress Semiconductor Corporation, for example, the company's 1400 employees each commit to fulfilling particular goals by specified dates. A computer tracks the status of these tasks and lets both management and the workforce know how work is proceeding. The result is what the company calls a "no excuses" work atmosphere: either the job gets done or it doesn't, with rewards passed out accordingly.

At the same time, the installation of MBO management practices in some companies has caused noticeable growing pains. First, employees used to "doing whatever the boss asked" can become more difficult to manage when given the opportunity to participate in goal-setting. Second, particular tasks can be linked too narrowly to specific rewards; employees may develop a "piece-work" attitude, devoting their attention to high-reward tasks and ignoring necessary, but low-reward work activities. Third, the work force may spend too much time (and paperwork) getting ready to work rather than actually working. The discussion of goals may prove more expensive to the company than the achievement of those goals. Fourth, employees driven by their own assigned goals may become selfish to the detriment of the group. Employees may actually practice secretive or subversive behaviors with regard to the group so that their individual achievements stand out.

These potential problems with MBO programs can be overcome by the MBO process itself. The desired form of organizational structures, reward systems, and employee interactions can all be stated as goals, then assigned appropriately throughout the organization. A manager, in other words, can be as responsible for how a group works as for how an engine works.

MANAGEMENT TIPS

Management by objectives helps to solve the "who's supposed to be doing what?" question in business. MBO programs succeed when a manager:

1. takes time to discuss the context and importance of work goals with employees.

2. negotiates goals for an individual employee based on that employee's skills, experience, and interest.

3. ties performance evaluation directly to goals accepted by the employee.

4. distributes rewards fairly according to goal fulfillment.

5. monitors the success of goal-setting.

6. uses results from goal-setting in redesigning organizational policies and procedures.

CHAPTER 9

HOW DO YOU RELATE?

*Motivators and
Your Social Life*

All people are involved in interpersonal trading or transacting.

Roberta Kent, 36, has worked as an accountant for seven companies in the past ten years. She is divorced and has one child, a teenage daughter.

One question I always have to answer about my resume involves my frequent changes in employers. Those changes have all been by my choice. I've never had to leave a job because of the quality of my work.

I do refuse, however, to work with childish people. I consider the office a place for adult, professional relationships. It's not a place for anger, pettiness, pouting, or shallow favoritism. Many of my most promising work experiences have turned out to be disappointing because of the maturity level of the people I work for or work with.

As my strong recommendation letters make clear, I'm not an unreasonable or difficult person to work with. But I do expect to be addressed civilly by my supervisor. I expect my work instructions to be given to me in a timely way. I feel that I have the right to point out aspects of my work environment that prevent me from performing up to my own standards. These are not unreasonable expectations.

I don't believe that the office is the appropriate place for one's social life. Therefore, I have kept my friendships separate from my career. Some of my co-workers may misunderstand my motives in this regard. I'm not unfriendly in the office, but I don't seek out non-workrelated conversation. I can't help but notice that some employees spend a large portion of the workday engaged in personal conversations, not work activities.

I'm secure in my present position. My supervisor has complimented me on the accuracy and thoroughness of my work. She gives me accounting projects in sufficient time for the kind of careful job I insist on doing. I'm somewhat troubled, however, by her behavior in staff meetings. She seems to yield to the often unreasonable suggestions of some of her employees as a way of winning their favor. This aspect of her management style disappoints me, although I have not yet told her so. I wish she would be a strong leader.

FOLLOW-UP INFORMATION

Roberta is one of three sisters and the only one to complete college. She maintains frequent contact with her sisters, who often express their admiration for her professional accomplishments. Other than her sisters and a few church friends, Roberta has few social contacts. After a painful divorce, Roberta Kent has had sole custody and financial responsibility for what she calls "a rebellious daughter."

Roberta's financial life is problematic. She tends to exhaust her savings during periods of unemployment between jobs. For the past five years, she has suffered from alcoholism, a condition she hides from those outside her family and for which she has not sought professional help.

MOTIVATORS AT WORK

Getting the best out of people involves understanding them. But what is a manager to do with a stiff, uncooperative Roberta Kent? Or, just as bad, with Charly, the office clown? Or Samantha, the earth-mother who spends all day, every day listening to everyone's domestic problems?

Although psychologist Eric Berne didn't direct his research toward business *per se*, his theories of Transactional Analysis (TA) have revolutionized the way managers observe and relate to their employees.

Berne suggests that all people are involved in interpersonal trading or transacting. When Roberta says, "Please don't disturb me," to Charly, the office clown, she has initiated half of an interpersonal transaction. When Charly responds, "You just can't take a joke, Roberta," he completes the transaction.

The Complete Transaction

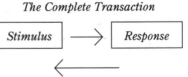

Feedback

Transactions, according to Berne, spring from portions of our personalities over which we have only limited control. Each of us carries within three "speakers" or subpersonalities able to assert themselves.

The Parent

This personality force is the sum total of all the advice and commands we've been given over the years by various controllers, including parents, teachers, religious leaders, older siblings, and other authority figures. Although they may no longer be physically present, they are still "there" inside us, telling us (and others) what to do.

The Parent within us tends to rely upon unquestioned maxims and principles. Some of these may be deeply prejudicial: "You can't trust those kinds of people" (with regard to gender, race, religion, or national background) and "You can't teach an old dog new tricks" (with regard to age).

Other Parent messages within us may be reruns of messages instilled by our own parents or other authority figures:

"Don't talk back."
"I'm only going to say this once."
"Do as you're told."
"I'm in charge here, not you."
"You don't want to get on my bad side."
"You'll be sorry if I have to get angry."
"If you lie to me, I'll never trust you again."

Although our Parent voice may not say such things so directly to business associates, we may communicate these essential messages in the way we react to others, particularly in moments of stress and crisis.

The Parent voice within can be viewed on a continuum from Nurturing (advice for the sake of growth) to Critical (advice for punishment). The Nurturing Parent communicates that bad actions may endanger the good person; the Critical Parent communicates that bad actions reveal the bad person.

Parent Continuum

Nurturing   *Critical*

$$\longleftarrow \quad \longrightarrow$$

In sum, the Parent portion of the personality emphasizes what "should" or "must" be done, as judged against a predetermined but often unexamined standard.

The Adult

The Adult portion of personality is reasonable and practical, but unemotional. The Adult examines causes, motives, and consequences of actions. The Adult makes plans, creates procedures, and functions within self-defined limits. The Adult takes responsibility for personal actions.

Roberta Kent, for example, is the consummate adult in her work behavior. She makes sure that each of her actions during the day is defensible by logical reasoning. She can explain exactly what she is doing, why, where, when, and for whom. She resists distraction from employees who do not have the same firm sense of purpose and direction. She leaves the employ of those companies where procedures and protocol are not maintained.

The Child

This final portion of the total personality is the source of emotional response. The Child casts aside logic and consequences in favor of natural feeling:

> "This excites me!"
> "It made me feel wonderful!"
> "He really hurt my feelings!"
> "I like her style."
> "I just enjoy working here."
> "I'm getting really frustrated."
> "I'm bored in my job."

The Child not only feels these emotions, but gives them high importance for determining follow-up action. "I'm getting really frustrated . . . so I'm going to quit." "He really hurt my feelings . . . so I'll pay him back." "I like her style . . . so I'll promote her."

Like the Parent, the Child can be described as a span of internal forces ranging from the Happy Child to the Destructive Child. The Happy Child acts on the basis of personal feelings, but does so in a way that is not harmful to the interests of others. The Destructive Child also acts on the basis of personal feelings, but harms the interests of others in the process.

Child Continuum

Happy   *Destructive*

Unlike the Adult, the Child force does not stop to consider causes, motives, or consequences before responding. Whether in joy or pain, the Child simply bursts out.

Parent-Adult-Child in Harmony

No one personality state is in itself ideal. The healthy personality allows all three internal forces to surface at appropriate times. We recognize these people as being "together."

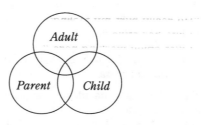

These are the people who have a strong sense of values (Parent force) but at the same time can listen well to consider alternatives (Adult force). All the while, they're good company for their spontaneity, humor, and sympathy (Child force).

MOTIVATING PARENT-DOMINATED EMPLOYEES

As described earlier, Parent-dominated people can be recognized by their reruns of unquestioned positions and prejudices. They may be proud of the fact that they "dig in their heels" when asked to do something they don't want to. Or, by the same Parent force, they may feel an absolute duty to proceed with a task far beyond their abilities.

Motivating this personality type always involves moving the person by degrees toward more Adult perceptions of the situation at hand. In the following dialogue between a manager and a Parent-dominated employee, notice how the manager emphasizes what *is* (Adult perception) to replace what *should be* (Critical Parent perception):

> *Manager: Jack, I'd like you to consider applying for the new government liaison position.*
>
> *Jack: Thanks, but I'm not much for taking plunges. Better safe than sorry.*
>
> *Manager: The new position would let you apply your many years of Pentagon experience.*
>
> *Jack: I'd rather let someone else try it first.*
>
> *Manager: I think you'd enjoy being in touch with top decisionmakers here at the company and in government.*
>
> *Jack: Well . . .*
>
> *Manager: And there's the pay. You could expect a significant raise.*

Jack eventually decides to apply for the job as his manager highlights more and more of the reasonable attractions of the position from an Adult perspective. The manager would have had much less motivational success by opposing Jack's Parent tendencies: "Jack, you're always afraid to try something new. You should be more ambitious." In this approach, the manager is playing Critical Parent (what's wrong, what should be). In so doing, the manager inadvertently magnifies Jack's own Parent responses: "Well, I think I should stick to what I know, not chase something new."

MOTIVATING ADULT-DOMINATED EMPLOYEES

Like Mr. Spock on "Star Trek," Adult-dominated employees can be logical and reasonable to the point of their own disadvantage. Roberta Kent, for example, is such a "good" employee (by her definition) that she can hardly find a company worthy enough to employ her or colleagues up to her standards. Too often, the Roberta Kents of corporate life end up as a footnote in an exit interview file: "Good performance potential, but poor interpersonal skills."

To motivate a Roberta Kent to more human and more productive work relations, a manager must awaken her Child personality component. Roberta, it appears, has been reserving this Child for personally destructive drinking binges after work. She "lets loose" only when others can't see her, then reverts to a rigid form of Adult behavior for her work life.

In the following conversation with Roberta, a manager emphasizes and validates feelings, not logical responses. In time, Roberta may learn that her feelings are not only appropriate but are valued in the workplace. With that realization will undoubtedly come her own acceptance of the feelings of others.

> *Manager: I was disappointed to see that the Executive Council cancelled the marketing project you were working on. How did you feel about the situation?*
> *Roberta: I understood from their memo to me that the project had to be cancelled because of regulatory changes. [Adult emphasis on reason]*
> *Manager: I got a copy of the same memo. How did you feel when you read it?*
> *Roberta: I don't know all of the facts, but I assume they made a logical decision.*

*Manager: But after all your work . . . To tell you the
truth, I got really angry to see them change
directions like this. How about you? [Discloses
feelings, invites her feelings]*

*Roberta: Well, it did make me feel that I had wasted
three weeks of work . . .*

Manager: That's understandable.

*Roberta: . . . and I was really frustrated that they
didn't let me know sooner about regulatory
changes. They had to know about them months
ago!*

*Manager: It is frustrating when top management isn't
doing their job. I hate it when the left hand doesn't
know what the right hand is doing.*

As this conversation proceeds, Roberta learns that
she can share her work-related feelings, both positive and
negative, with her manager. In time, she may broaden her
network of work associates to include others she trusts
with her feelings. One of these people may eventually help
her take steps to control her alcoholism, a personality
disease not unrelated to her suppressed Child responses.

MOTIVATING CHILD-DOMINATED EMPLOYEES

Finally, there's Charly, the office clown—superbly gifted
in social skills, but a time-waster for himself and for others. Acting from his inner Child, Charly spends his entire
day expressing his own emotions and sympathizing with
the emotions of others. It's hard to dislike Charly—he's
personable in the extreme. But likeability isn't the issue
when work has to get done.

A manager probably won't have much luck approach-
ing Charly with strong Parent messages. The Child, after
all, stands in rebellion against the Parent. Charly behaves
as he does to "get a little life into the office, put a bit of

fun back in the day." There is little hope that Charly will be motivated to more productive behavior by a series of "shoulds" in the form of a Parent message from manager.

Instead, the manager tries in the following dialogue to move Charly toward more Adult behavior. The manager's emphasis is on what *is*, without explicitly criticizing Charly and specifying a list of "shoulds" for him.

> *Manager: I noticed your weekly report wasn't in by 10:00 a.m. yesterday.*
>
> *Charly: Oops, there. Barbara, Frank, and I got talking about the rumor that headquarters will be relocated to Toledo. Can you imagine that? That city's motto is, "What's the point?"*
>
> *Manager: I got Barbara and Frank's reports on time. I didn't get yours.*
>
> *Charly: Day late and a dollar short. My life story.*
>
> *Manager: This isn't the first late report, Charly. What's the problem?*
>
> *Charly: No problem. Like I say, there are two kinds of time—company time and Charly time.*
>
> *Manager: My boss only pays attention to company time. What keeps you from getting your work in on time?*
>
> *Charly: Nothing particular. Just day-to-day stuff, I guess.*
>
> *Manager: Such as?*

As this conversation proceeds, Charly is forced off his routine of one-liners to confront his Child behavior and its results. The manager at no time lectures Charly on what should be done; instead, the emphasis is on what *is* happening and what may be causing it. Charly the Child may be ready to rebel against and reject Parent forces, but he is ill-armed to refute the Adult facts of his work life. With persistence on the manager's part, Charly can regain his usefulness as an employee without losing his charm as a person.

MANAGEMENT TIPS

Employees exhibiting Parent-, Adult-, or Child-dominated behavior in the workplace can be motivated to more productive work habits.

1. Parent-dominated employees resist original thinking and perpetuate stereotypes in their work and relationships. Use Adult rationality and logic to persuade such people that their limitations of self and others are both unnecessary and disadvantageous.

2. Adult-dominated employees lose the zest of work challenges and perform poorly in groups. Demonstrate to such people that feelings, appropriately expressed, are natural and valuable in the workplace.

3. Child-dominated employees base their actions primarily on feeling. Showing them what they should be doing (Parent perspective) is often less effective than pointing out the actual results of their behavior (Adult perspective).

CHAPTER 10

WHAT'S YOUR GAME?

*Motivators and
Manipulation*

Psychological games waste the energies of well-intentioned employees.

n the following dialogue, a supervisor talks with Ralph Calvert, 24, an account executive responsible for a major fast food advertising account.

> *Calvert: As I told you before, I'm under a lot of pressure from Burger Boys. They want their ads right up there with the national chains.*
>
> *Supervisor: They want TV ads?*
>
> *Calvert: Yes, but I just finished buttoning up the big print ad campaign for them—you know, the Better Burger ads. What are we supposed to do, just trash that hard work?*
>
> *Supervisor: I guess that depends on what the client is willing to pay for.*
>
> *Calvert: Yes, but they haven't given the print campaign a chance to work.*
>
> *Supervisor: Have you discussed this with them, Ralph?*
>
> *Calvert: Yes, I've tried to on several occasions, but all they can talk about is television advertising.*
>
> *Supervisor: Well, it seems obvious to me that your clients wants some leadership from you on a new kind of ad campaign in a different medium.*

> *Calvert: Yes, but how do I get them to give the Better
>   Burgers ads a fair chance?*
> *Supervisor: I guess it's your call, Ralph. I don't seem
>   to be helping very much.*

FOLLOW-UP INFORMATION ON RALPH CALVERT

Ralph comes from a family of very successful professionals. His mother is a prominent neurologist, his father an
attorney. Vincent, Ralph's older brother, is a regional di-
rector for the Environmental Protection Agency.

Ralph's mother and father convinced Ralph at an early
age that he was no Vincent. In high school and college,
Ralph's test scores and grades were well below Vincent's.
Ralph struggled for his BA; Vincent breezed through an
MBA at Wharton. It went on and on. Vincent owned his
home, Ralph rented; Vincent had married Ms. Perfect,
Ralph was dating on and off; Vincent drove a Porsche,
Ralph a Toyota.

Ralph understood that a dark cloud seemed to move
wherever he moved. He had come to expect it at the most
important moments of his personal life and career. The
Better Burger print campaign was his first big project in
advertising. But right on schedule, the dark cloud moves
in. The clients want to change to television ads.

MOTIVATORS AT WORK

Most of us probably participated in a childhood game, "Bug
the Sub," when a substitute teacher took over class for
the day. Game behaviors were predictable for our up-
roarious classmates, and total scoring depended on the
outcome by the end of the day: highest points for the
substitute's hysterical tears, less for harangues, calls for
the principal's assistance, and threats to call parents.

For some of us, the playing of psychological games
didn't end with elementary school. We may still have rou-

tinized behaviors that, consciously or subconsciously, we play out in our business lives.

In the opening scenario, Ralph Calvert is playing one of the most familiar of such games—"Yes, but." Like all psychological games, "Yes, but" has three characteristics.

1. The moves are ritualized and repetitious on the part of the game initiator. No matter what the supervisor says, Ralph will respond with an explanation beginning with "Yes, but."

2. The game has a surface level and a hidden level. At the surface level, Ralph seems sincere in his request for his supervisor's advice. But at a hidden level, the game is already decided. Ralph will accept none of the supervisor's ideas and, in fact, is not even interested in those ideas.

3. The game empowers the initiator by frustrating the other player. Ralph draws his game victory not from the value of his supervisor's advice but from the supervisor's eventual inability to offer advice. In transactional terms (see Chapter 9), Ralph the Child overpowers the Supervisor Parent by reducing him to silence. (A similar behavior can be observed in the child who screams "I want it!" over and over until the parent quits objecting and gives in.)

Psychological games waste the energies of well-intentioned employees. Ralph's supervisor, for example, didn't recognize that he was caught in a psychological game. He worked hard, therefore, to come up with alternatives, explanations, and possibilities for Ralph. The supervisor didn't understand that the goal of the game was his frustration, not his help. In many companies, psychological games on the part of key employees lead to unnecessary meetings, memos, letters, and reports, all wasted.

Just as harmful, however, are the effects of psychological gaming on the game player. In our opening scenario, Ralph is rehearsing a game pattern he has probably played since childhood. (Psychologists believe, in fact, that lifelong psychological games usually begin in childhood.) Success breeds success, and with each repetition of his "Yes, but" game Ralph becomes more and more its master. He learns, that is, how to initiate the game so subtly that not even his closest associates realize they are caught in a no-win situation until it is too late.

In time, therefore, game players become increasingly dangerous to their organizations. The same games that block conversation can end up blocking production schedules and development plans. The size of a game player's "win," after all, is in direct relation to the total amount of frustration he produces.

RECOGNIZING PSYCHOLOGICAL GAMING

Managers who attempt to motivate their employees by the various methods described in these chapters may sometimes find even their most intensive efforts backfiring. The culprit may be a psychological game. Recognize its presence by the game player's recurring behaviors that suggest a "no-win" course for your efforts. The sooner you spot this "no-win" horizon, the sooner you can redirect your effort to end the game.

MOTIVATING PSYCHOLOGICAL GAME-PLAYERS

The essence of the psychological game lies in the player's need to frustrate you. Understanding the nature of that perverse need is the first necessary step for motivating the game player to more productive interaction.

Game-players usually have a long history of unsuccessful relations with authority figures. In some cases, an authority figure always imposes his or her will. In other cases, the authority figure withholds needed affection.

The game-player, because he cannot get what he wants from the authority figure, must psychologically remove the authority figure's importance. In game-playing conversations, this can best be accomplished by reducing the authority figure to frustrated silence (the direct opposite, that is, of authoritative speaking). In game-playing actions, the goals of the organization are subverted by apparently innocent delays, misplaced documents, and ambiguous directions.

A manager cannot literally give in to a game-player's attempts to psychologically assassinate authority figures. But a manager can supply in a positive way what a game-player seeks in a negative way. In other words, a manager can help a game-player find enough self-importance and recognition so that game-playing becomes unnecessary.

In the opening scenario, for example, Ralph's supervisor could have realized early on that Ralph would "yes, but" all of his suggestions. Instead of playing Ralph's game, the supervisor could have gone directly to the heart of Ralph's problem: his felt lack of recognition and success. Notice in this revised conversation how the supervisor avoids Ralph's game and at the same time motivates him to new levels of achievement.

> *Calvert: As I told you before, I'm under a lot of pressure from Burger Boys. They want their ads right up there with the national chains.*
> *Supervisor: They want TV ads?*
> *Calvert: Yes, but I just finished buttoning up the big print ad campaign for them—you know, the Better Burger ads. What are we supposed to do, just trash that hard work?*
> *Supervisor (realizing the beginning of the "yes, but" game): Ralph, let's stop right here. What's really bothering you about the Burger Boys account?*
> *Calvert: What do you mean?*
> *Supervisor: How do you feel about the whole matter?*
> *Calvert: Kind of kicked around, I guess.*
> *Supervisor: Kicked around?*
> *Calvert: Yeah, I do my best for these guys, and they pull the rug out from under me. I thought I could trust them.*
> *Supervisor: So what would make you feel better about things?*

Calvert: I don't know.

Supervisor: Come on, Ralph. You said this whole thing made you feel lousy. So what would make you feel better?

Calvert: It sounds stupid, but I'd love to get revenge. See them stuck without an ad campaign.

Supervisor: And how does that help you?

Calvert: Well, it doesn't help me financially, but it would sure make me feel better.

Supervisor: So there's your choice, Ralph. You can go on resisting their desire for TV ads and get your revenge. Or you can skip the revenge and succeed financially. [Note here that the manager doesn't take the role of an authority figure telling Ralph what to do.]

Calvert: (laughs) The revenge is tempting, but I'd rather have the money, I guess.

The supervisor concludes by praising that choice and reminding Ralph how valuable his work is for the company.

MANAGEMENT TIPS

By adulthood, some employees have become masters at elaborate psychological games intended to make the game partner feel frustrated, helpless, guilty, or insignificant. Managers can avoid the dangerous effects of game-playing in their organizations in these ways:

1. Recognize psychological games by repetitious behavior on the part of the game player and a "no-win" future for the conversation or course of actions.

2. Remove the game-player from key roles where his actions can subvert organizational goals.

3. Motivate the game-player to more productive behavior by providing in a positive way the attention, recognition, or understanding he perversely seeks through games.

A FINAL NOTE

We should not look upon psychological game-players as sociopaths or social pariahs. To some extent, we all engage in some forms of manipulative "game" behavior in our personal or professional lives. What we can watch for in ourselves and in others is that point at which psychological games become personally and organizationally destructive. Then the game's over—or should be.

CONCLUSION

With hiring and training costs rising precipitously in most companies, there has never been a better time to get the most from the employees you have. Such motivation, as we have seen, begins with a single principle: understand the individual you seek to motivate.

Using scenarios, we have seen how different individuals respond to quite different motivators. Gathered here for ease of reference are abbreviated versions of the specific management tips offered in each chapter. Put these suggestions where they belong—at work for you!

Motivation by Need Hierarchy

1. Motivators depend directly on what an employee thinks he or she needs.
2. Those needs can be discerned by a manager through listening and observing.
3. Employees' needs are hierarchical: lower-stage needs must be met before higher needs can be addressed.
4. The manager's needs may be quite different from the employee's needs.

Motivation by Expectancy

1. Employees will devote more effort to achieving goals that they think are attainable.
2. Such effort may fall off when the achievement of the goal seems certain.

3. For maximum motivation, employees must value the rewards they expect to receive.

Motivation by Equity

1. Managers must know what jobs, titles, and salaries employees are likely to use for comparison.
2. Managers must structure organizations to prevent unproductive comparisons.
3. Managers can control information flow to influence comparison.
4. Managers can use expectancy rewards to reduce the impact of unavoidable comparisons.

Motivation by Job Satisfaction

1. Managers should beware of the Hawthorne Effect, in which any group of employees highlighted for special attention will respond with temporarily increased productivity.
2. Poor work conditions can limit the capacity of workers to perform.
3. The elimination of poor work conditions does not automatically create a satisfying and motivating work climate.
4. Managers should not impose their motivational priorities on their employees.

Motivation by Management Assumptions

1. Managers should ask employees what they think about business problems.
2. Managers should encourage discussion and evaluation.
3. Managers should welcome tentative judgments and speculative ideas.
4. Employees should be thanked and trusted.
5. Employees should be freed to develop individual skills for use in the company.
6. Employees should be involved in the evaluation of their work.

Motivation by Group Attitudes

1. Managers should listen to the company grapevine to determine thoughts and feelings of employees.
2. Managers should act promptly to counter false rumors and incorrect information.
3. Managers should structure their organizations to prevent disadvantageous power groups and cliques.

Motivation by Self-perception

1. Managers should treat employees as "OK" individuals.
2. Managers should focus on actions, not personalities, when delivering evaluations.
3. Managers should emphasize and plan for professional growth opportunities for employees.
4. Managers should resist scapegoating and promote team consciousness.
5. Managers should praise and reward employees fairly.
6. Managers should be able to forgive and forget when appropriate.

Motivation by Objectives

1. Managers should take time to discuss the context and importance of work goals with employees.
2. Managers should negotiate goals for an individual employee based on skills, experience, and interest.
3. Managers should tie performance evaluations directly to goals accepted by the employee.
4. Managers should distribute rewards fairly according to goal fulfillment.

Motivation by Social Transaction

1. Managers can use Adult rationality and logic to persuade Parent-dominated employees of the value of original thinking and risk-taking.
2. Managers can emphasize the appropriate expression of feeling in the workplace to Adult-dominated employees who have lost the zest of work challenges.

3. Managers can influence the actions of Child-dominated employees by showing them the results of their actions.

Motivation and Psychological Games

1. Managers can recognize game-players by their repetitious behavior and the presence of a "no-win" scenario for their interactions.
2. Managers should remove game-players from positions crucial to organizational success.
3. Managers can use attention, recognition, and understanding to motivate game-players to more productive behavior.

ADDITIONAL READINGS

For additional information on this topic, please refer to the
following resources.

Bernardin, H. John and Richard W. Beatty. *Performance
Appraisal: Assessing Human Behavior at Work*. Boston:
Kent Publishing Company, 1984.

Champagne, Paul J. *Motivation Strategies for Performance
and Productivity: A Guide to Human Resource Development*. New York: Quorum Books, 1989.

Cherrington, David J. *Organizational Behavior: Management of Individual and Organizational Performance*.
Boston: Allyn and Bacon, 1989.

Hersey, Paul and Kenneth H. Blanchard. *Management of
Organizational Behavior: Utilizing Human Resources*,
5th ed. Englewood Cliffs: Prentice Hall, 1988.

Herzberg, Frederick. *Work and the Nature of Man*.
Cleveland: World Publishing Company, 1966.

Herzberg, Frederick, Bernard Mausner, and Barbara
Snyderman. *The Motivation to Work*. New York: John
Wiley, 1959.

Higgens, James M. *The Management Challenge: An Intro-
duction to Management*. New York: MacMillan, 1991.

Kovach, Kenneth A. "What Motivates Employees? Workers and Supervisors Give Different Answers," *Business
Horizons.*, September-October 1987, pp. 58–65.

Lawler, Edward E. *Motivation in Work Organizations*.
Monterey: Brooks/Cole Publishing Company, 1963.

Maslow, Abraham H. *Motivation and Personality*, 2nd ed.
New York: Harper & Row, 1970.

Macarov, David. *Incentives to Work*. San Francisco: Jossey-Bass, 1970.

McClelland, David. *The Achieving Society*. New York: Van Nostrand Reinhold, 1961.

Morf, Martin. *Optimizing Work Performance: A Look Beyond the Bottom Line*. New York: Quorum Books, 1986.

Murrell, Hywell. *Motivation at Work*. London: Methlen, 1976.

Nadler, David A. and Edward L. Lawler, III. "Motivation: A Diagnostic Approach," in J. Richard and Hackman, Edward E. Lawler, and Lyman W. Porter, eds. *Perspectives on Behavior in Organizations*, 2nd ed. New York: McGraw-Hill, 1983, pp. 67–78.

Pinder, Craig C. *Work Motivation: Theories, Issues and Applications*. Glenview, Ill: Scott, Foresman, 1984.

Quick, Thomas L. *Quick Solutions: 500 People Problems Managers Face & How to Solve Them*. New York: John Wiley & Sons, 1987.

Robins, Stephen P. *Management*. Englewood Cliffs: Prentice Hall, 1991.

Steers, Richard. *Motivation and Work Behavior*. New York: McGraw Hill, 1983.

Vroom, Victor H. *Work and Motivation*. New York: John Wiley, 1964.

Yukl, Gary. *Skills for Managers and Leaders*. Englewood Cliffs: Prentice Hall, 1990.

Zaleznik, Abraham. *The Motivation, Productivity and Satisfaction of Workers: A Prediction Study*. Boston: Harvard University, Division of Research, Graduate School of Business Administration, 1954.

INDEX